The Siege of White Deer Park

Adder could see nothing of his attacker. He was unable to turn to look behind, and the pressure was so great on his body that he thought his bones might break. There were no animals in the Park who ate snake and so Adder was in no doubt that he was trapped either by a human foot, or, more likely, by the very creature he had intended himself to surprise. There was a momentary easing of the pressure and Adder at once tried to turn. As soon as he moved, a huge paw swung round and patted at his head. Luckily for him the claws were retracted.

The Siege of White Deer Park

Colin Dann

Illustrated by Terry Riley

RED FOX

A Red Fox Book

Published by Random House Children's Books
20 Vauxhall Bridge Road, London SW1V 2SA

A division of Random House UK Ltd

London Melbourne Sydney Auckland
Johannesburg and agencies throughout the world

First published by Hutchinson Children's Books 1985
Beaver edition 1986
Reprinted 1986, 1987, 1988 and 1990
Red Fox edition 1991
Reprinted 1991
This edition 1992

5 7 9 10 8 6

Printed and bound in Great Britain by
Cox & Wyman Ltd, Reading, Berkshire

RANDOM HOUSE UK Limited Reg. No. 954009

ISBN 0 09 920541 6

Contents

**For Sarah, Rachael, David
and Ruth**

—1—
What Sort of Creature?

In the Nature Reserve of White Deer Park the animals were looking forward to the bustle of Spring. It was the end of February and dead Winter's grasp was loosening little by little with each spell of sunshine. The survivors of the band of beasts and birds who had travelled to the haven of the Park from their destroyed home in Farthing Wood had passed their third winter in the confines of the Reserve. Only a few still survived. The short life spans of most had run their course. But now their descendants populated the Park, and they knew no other home. These voles and mice, hedgehogs, rabbits and hares mingled and mated as natives with others of their kind whose forefathers had always lived within the Park's boundaries. Yet they were still conscious of a sort of allegiance to the few stalwarts of the old Farthing Wood community who remained alive.

Foremost among these were the Farthing Wood Fox and his mate Vixen, venerated almost as mythical beings to whom the animals turned for advice and counsel. They were the doyens of the Park's inhabitants, along with the aged Great Stag who was still supreme among the deer herd. Fox's oldest companion, Badger, was also a counsellor who tried to promote harmony between birds and beasts where it was feasible within their own natural order. Badger was very ancient now and never strayed far from his own set. He was slow, dim-sighted and rather feeble, but his kindly ways made him, if less respected, more loved even than Fox.

Tawny Owl, Adder, Toad, Weasel and Whistler the heron still lived and were occasional companions of Badger's extreme old age. But the old creature missed Mole, who had been his special friend. Mole's offspring – the result of his union with Mirthful, a female born in the Reserve – tended to live their own lives. So Badger suffered the loss of the wonderful bond that had existed between the two underground dwellers. Mole's allotted span of existence had reached its end during the winter. As he had lived, so he died – underground. His home had become his grave, and his tiny body went unnoticed in the labyrinth of tunnels. But he was remembered and mourned.

The descendants of Fox and Vixen now stretched almost to the fourth generation, for in the spring the cubs of their grandchildren would be born. From their own first litter Friendly and Charmer survived. Their cub Bold, who had left the Reserve and died outside it, had mated with Whisper who had journeyed to the Park for the safe birth of her own offspring. Now they, too, would become parents. So each season the Farthing Wood lineage was extended.

Badger and Tawny Owl had never paired off in their second home. They were too old and set in their ways – at least, so they said. As for Adder, who vanished altogether for long periods – well, no one was quite sure about him . . . .

It was dusk on one of the last days of February when the first signs of some strange influence in their lives appeared to one of the old comrades from Farthing Wood. Tawny Owl had been quartering the Park's boundaries where these adjoined the open downland. He noticed an unusual number of rabbits converging on a hole scraped under part of the fencing. The timid animals were jostling and bumping each other in their attempts to reach this entrance to the Reserve before their fellows.

'Hm,' mused Owl. 'This is odd. What's their hurry, I wonder?' He was not thinking of the possibilities for himself in this sudden abundance of food. His first thought was for the cause of their fright. He flew out of the Park a little way, following the rabbits' trail backwards – all of the time expecting to discover what was driving them. But he saw nothing, however much his night eyes scanned the ground.

'*Something* scared them,' he murmured to himself. 'Yet why haven't they dived for their burrows?' Tawny Owl knew all about the behaviour of rabbits.

He flew back and hooted a question at them. 'What's all the fuss about?'

Some of the animals looked up but, when they saw the owl, they scuttled ahead even faster. They were certainly not going to stop still to talk to a hunter! And, by the time Tawny Owl remembered his stomach, they had disappeared into the undergrowth.

He perched in an ash tree and pondered, his great round eyes staring unseeingly through the bare branches. He rustled his brown wings.

'No point brooding on it,' he muttered. 'Things reveal themselves eventually.' He flew off on his noiseless flight into the gathering darkness.

A few days later, again in the evening, Fox and Vixen were emerging from their den to go foraging. In the winter months there was often carrion to be found and recently they had been subsisting chiefly on that. Fox paused as a clatter of wings broke the stillness of their home wood.

'Pigeons,' he remarked.

But there were other noises. Birds' cries, and the sounds of sudden movements in the tree-tops as many took to flight, made the pair of foxes listen intently. There was a general disturbance that went on for some minutes.

'The whole wood's been alarmed,' said Vixen. She stayed close to her bolt-hole in case of trouble.

Fox gazed fixedly at the night sky. At last he said: 'I think I see what it is.'

Vixen waited for him to explain. He was still looking up through the fretwork of naked branches.

'Yes,' he said. 'I'm sure of it.'

'Well – what?' Vixen prompted, a little impatiently.

'There are a lot of birds flying in from beyond the Park. They seem to be wheeling about, uncertain where to go. They must have unsettled those at roost here.'

'They sound very panicky,' Vixen observed.

The foxes watched a while longer. Eventually many of the birds from outside found perches in the Reserve.

Others flew onwards, and gradually quietness was restored. Fox and Vixen went on their way.

Occurrences such as these became more frequent in the ensuing weeks. All the inhabitants of the Park became aware that something, as yet unknown, was bringing change to their little world. Animals from all over the countryside came flooding into the Park. Sometimes the creatures stayed; sometimes they passed right through or overhead; sometimes they returned again whence they had come. But it was obvious that the wildlife around was in a state of real alarm, and these continual movements to and fro brought an atmosphere of disquiet to the Nature Reserve. Weasel, running through the carpet of Dog's Mercury under the beech trees, noticed a sudden increase in the numbers of wood mice. These mice appeared to have thrown their inbred caution to the winds – most of them were running about quite openly, inviting themselves to be taken. Weasel was not one to refuse the offer and he had quite a field day or, rather, night. It was only later that he realized that the mice had been thrown into a state of panic by the arrival of dozens of hunting stoats and weasels like himself, who were closing in on their quarry from every direction. The poor mice simply did not know where to run next. But where had these hunting cousins of his suddenly appeared from? They were certainly not the ordinary inhabitants of White Deer Park.

Squirrel and his relatives found themselves competing for their hoards of autumn-buried acorns and beech mast with strangers from elsewhere who watched where they dug and stole where they could.

Hare's first-born, Leveret, who was still called so by his Farthing Wood friends from old association (though he had for long now been an adult) saw more of his own kind running through the dead grass and bracken than he had ever done since his arrival in White Deer Park.

Finally the friends began to gather to compare their opinions. It was now March and a shimmer of green was slowly spreading through the Park. New grass, tentative leaves on hawthorn and hazel, and ripening sycamore and chestnut buds gave glad signs to the animals that Winter was over. But they were puzzled and a little worried by the recent influxes.

'Where do they come from?' asked Squirrel.

'What's bringing them here?' asked Leveret.

Badger had no comment to make. He was only acquainted with the facts by hearsay. He had seen nothing himself.

'It's as if they've been driven here,' Tawny Owl said.

Fox had been doing a lot of thinking. 'You could be right, Owl,' he remarked. 'Birds and beasts are being driven here to the Reserve in the hope of shelter and then – '

'Finding themselves cornered?' Vixen broke in.

'Exactly! Then they'd be ripe for rounding up. It's like part of a deliberate plan by some clever creature.'

'Or creatures,' Weasel observed.

'Yes,' said Fox. 'It couldn't be just one. Unless . . .'

'Unless of the human variety,' finished Whistler the heron drily.

'Wouldn't make sense,' Tawny Owl contradicted him. 'What purpose could there be in this for Man?'

'How should we know?' asked Friendly, Fox's son. 'Who else is so clever?'

'I don't like this rounding up idea,' Leveret said nervously. 'It stands to reason – *we'd* be caught up in it too.'

They fell silent while they digested the implications of this.

'From what you say, Fox,' Badger wheezed, 'it sounds as if some animal or other is planning to use the Park as a sort of larder.'

Fox looked at him. 'You've gone straight to the point, Badger. But what sort of creature . . . .' he muttered inconclusively.

'A sort of creature *we* know nothing about,' said Owl.

'The deer are very uneasy,' put in Vixen. 'You can tell they sense something.'

'It's horrible waiting around,' said Charmer, her daughter, 'for this . . . this . . . *Something* to make an appearance. There are young to be born and looked after.'

'We mustn't get too jittery,' said Fox. 'Perhaps there *is* no "Something". There might be a more simple explanation. And a less alarming one.' But he could not convince himself.

Tawny Owl said, 'We mustn't fool ourselves either, Fox. We should prepare for the worst.'

'That's very helpful,' remarked Weasel sarcastically.

'I meant it for the best,' Owl defended himself. 'We don't want to be caught napping, do we?'

'No, but there's a reasonable chance in your case,' Weasel murmured wickedly. It was well known that Tawny Owl spent most of the daylight hours dozing. Owl pretended not to hear.

'Oh!' exclaimed Fox. 'How I wish our brave Kestrel was still around to do some scouting for us!'

'Yes,' said Whistler the heron. 'If anyone could have spotted the danger he could have done. But can I be of any service? I don't have Kestrel's piercing vision, but I *do* have wings, and there's a deal to be seen from the air which you creatures would likely miss.'

'Of course,' said Fox. 'Thank you. Any help is most welcome.'

'You know long flights are awkward with your bad wing,' Tawny Owl pointed out to the heron. He referred to the bird's old wound from a badly aimed bullet, which had caused him more trouble as he grew older. 'It had better be me.'

Whistler, whose name derived from the noise this wing made as it flapped through the air, knew perfectly well that Owl felt he had lost face by not offering his services first. But he was too polite to mention it. 'That's all right,' he said. 'I know you night birds have to catch up on your sleep while my sort are active.'

His intended tact misfired. Tawny Owl's feelings were hurt. He was very conscious that his advancing age made him sleep longer than he used to. His feathers ruffled indignantly.

'Nonsense!' he said. 'I'm quite capable of flying by day. And more accurately than you, I might add.'

'As you say, old friend,' Whistler said readily with his constant good humour. He was quite unaffected by Owl's sharp retort.

'We'll share the search then.'

'Very well,' replied Owl huffily.

Weasel looked at Owl with distaste. 'He gets worse as he gets older,' he murmured to himself.

— 2 —

The Pond is Deserted

The two birds made long flights over the surrounding area; the heron by day, the owl by night. Neither was able to see anything that might explain the recent developments. But some of the creatures who had taken refuge within the Reserve talked to the animals they met there. Word spread of a large, fierce beast who made raids in the night. No animal had seen it and survived, so none of the refugees could give even the vaguest description of it. There were rumours of terrible slaughter. Tales of its unnerving hunting skills were rife. It could climb; it could swim; it could catch creatures underground. Some even suspected it could fly, since birds also suffered from its depredations. Soon the whole Park was in a state of suspense.

But it was Spring and, despite the suspense, the activities of Spring went on. Pairing and mating, nest-building and preparing dens for imminent births overrode any other consideration. For a while the threat of the unknown seemed to recede. Then, with startling suddenness, a change in the usual absorbing routine shocked the animals out of their preoccupation. In the midst of their mating season, the colony of Edible Frogs made a mass exodus from their pond. They were not content to hide themselves in the waterside vegetation. They hopped away in all directions as far as they could go, apparently desperate to get right away from the pond. Other aquatic creatures such as newts were seen in great numbers leaving the pond, and the ducks, coots and moorhens who had built their nests on or near the water deserted them entirely. It was obvious that something very alarming had happened to drive them away. The animals and birds did not need to ask each other what this could be. They knew. The Beast had arrived in the Park.

Toad, who had acted as guide to the Farthing Wood animals on their long journey to White Deer Park, was eager to talk to Fox. He had not been in the water himself when the eruption of the Edible Frogs from the pond had occurred. But he had witnessed their panic.

'It was pandemonium,' he told Fox. 'They couldn't scramble away fast enough from that water. There was something *in* the pond.'

'Did you see what it was?' Fox asked quickly.

'No, no. It was too dark for that,' replied Toad. 'But I didn't want to stay around myself to find out!'

'Of course not. I can well see why.'

'I don't know what the Frogs will do now,' Toad croaked. 'The pond is their gathering point. How can they carry on their lives now – and in the middle of the most important time of the year?'

'I wonder how any of us will cope,' Fox returned. 'You can't deal with something unseen.'

'I'd like to stay around here for a while if I may?' Toad murmured. 'There's comfort in company and I haven't seen Badger in a long while.'

Fox spoke quietly: 'I'm afraid he's failing, Toad, little by little. We're all much older than we were, but Badger seems to live in his own little world. He only does what's necessary – can't be bothered with anything else.'

'I think Mole's sadly missed,' Toad murmured. 'And Kestrel too. What an acrobat *he* was in the sky! But our old life, back in the Wood, and the great trek here that seemed as if it would go on for ever – doesn't it seem so long ago?'

'An age,' Fox agreed. 'Vixen and I often talk about the past. A sign of *our* age, no doubt,' he mocked himself.

'Yes. We always overcame troubles together before, didn't we?' Toad went on. 'But, you know, this new menace – I have a feeling it may be too much for us.'

After this, life in the Reserve went on as if on tiptoe. The whole community held its breath – and waited. One morning the remains of three adult rabbits were found close together under some blackthorn. It was obvious this was not the work of a fox. The other rabbits spoke of a hint of soft footfalls around their burrows. As usual they had seen nothing. But each of them seemed to have been aware of a Presence.

At intervals other carcasses were discovered. Their killer had great stealth and cunning. It was never seen during the day, and at night, although every animal and bird stayed alert for it, nothing positive was heard.

The inhabitants of White Deer Park, many of whom were chiefly nocturnal in their habits, began to feel as if they were under siege. Yet they had to eat. They went about in fear and trepidation, trying to stay as close to their homes as possible. But deaths still occurred. The mystery continued to hang balefully over the Reserve.

The creature's amazing silence was a constant talking point. The hunters among the Park's population began to feel a sort of grudging respect for its expertise. Some of the young foxes harboured ideas of emulating its methods.

'That sort of skill would make any animal the most respected of predators,' remarked one youngster, a nephew of Friendly's called Husky.

'Do you admire it?' his uncle enquired.

'Of course. Don't you? If I were like that I'd be the envy of all.'

'You'd have to learn a little more quietness then,' Friendly chaffed him. The point was not lost on his young relative who was something of a chatterer. 'And,' he went on, 'can you climb trees?'

'I can climb a bit,' the youngster declared. 'I'm not sure about trees.'

While this conversation was proceeding, the elders of the Farthing Wood community were meeting specifically to discuss the threat from the super-predator. The talk seemed to go round and round in circles, without anything being resolved. At last Badger, who had held his peace for most of the time, murmured, 'I can't help thinking of cats.'

'What? What did you say, Badger?' Fox asked sharply.

'Well, you see, Fox,' Badger went on in his rather quavery voice, 'I'm reminded of Ginger Cat. I spent a lot of time with him in the Warden's home after my accident. You'll remember that winter when I hurt my –'

'Yes, yes,' Fox cut in hurriedly. He knew how Badger was apt to wander off the point. 'We all recall Ginger Cat. Now what about him?'

'Well, the thing that struck me most about *him* was his stealth,' Badger explained. 'He could be so quiet in his movements, you wouldn't know he was about. And . . . and . . . he could *climb* like anything. So I wonder if this stranger in our midst might be a cat?'

'Oh, Badger, don't be absurd!' Tawny Owl scoffed. 'How could a cat have slaughtered as this beast has done? It wouldn't have the strength.'

'I didn't necessarily mean a cat like the Warden's cat,' Badger continued doggedly. 'But – er – another sort of cat . . . .'

Weasel said: 'It makes sense, doesn't it, Fox?'

'I don't know,' said Fox. 'What other sorts of cats are there?'

None of them had an answer to that.

'It's *not* a cat,' Tawny Owl declared peremptorily. 'It's a larger animal altogether.'

'But if it's so large, Owl,' Weasel said cheekily, 'why haven't you been able to spot it?'

Tawny Owl looked awkward. 'I don't know,' he said, and shuffled his feet. 'But Whistler looked too,' he added quickly as if that helped his argument which, of course, it did not.

'The fact is,' said Toad, 'we're all completely in the dark. And we shall remain in the dark until one of us – or another animal – comes face to face with the creature.'

'If that should happen, he won't live to tell the tale,' Fox reminded him.

'He might – if he had wings,' Toad suggested.

'Wings haven't been of much use so far,' Whistler said. 'Birds have been taken from their nests.'

'Then the bird in question should remain in the air,' Toad answered.

'I think Toad has something,' Vixen remarked. 'Another search should be made. Tawny Owl and Whistler didn't actually search the Reserve itself because the beast was believed to be outside it.'

'Very true,' said Fox. 'No use looking by day, though. It keeps itself well hidden. Owl, if you were very clever and very quiet, you might catch a glimpse of it. It has to hunt.'

'Oh, I can match the beast itself for quietness,' Tawny Owl boasted. 'No question of that. My flight is utterly noiseless. You see, my wing feathers – '

'Yes, we're all aware of your abilities,' Weasel cut in, rather sourly.

'Will you have another try?' Fox asked hurriedly, before Owl reacted.

'I certainly will,' the bird answered at once. He was delighted to be relied upon, and flattered by Fox's confidence in him.

'I still think it's a creature of the feline type,' Badger muttered obstinately.

Tawny Owl stared at him. His hooked beak opened on a retort, but he closed it again without speaking. He would very soon prove Badger wrong about that.

The gathering began to break up, when Fox suddenly asked: 'Has anyone seen Adder?'

It appeared that none of them had. Toad was usually the first to set eyes on him in the spring, for they often hibernated together. But even he had no idea where he was.

'I don't like to leave him out of our discussion,' Fox remarked. 'But he knows where *we* are so it's easier for him to seek us out.'

'Perhaps now it's warmer he'll turn up soon?' suggested Whistler.

'Huh! I suppose he might deign to show himself,' Weasel retorted. 'But as time goes by Adder gets crustier and crustier or, perhaps I should say in his case, scalier and scalier.'

'He'll be around,' Toad affirmed. 'I think I know him better than you do, Weasel. You've always taken his offhand manner too much to heart. It's just his way. After all, he is a snake, not a warm-blooded mammal. And I can tell you, he's just as loyal as any of us.'

The little group split up and went about their own concerns. As it turned out, talking about Adder seemed, though quite by chance, to hasten his arrival. The very next day Vixen found him coiled up by the entrance to her earth.

'Ah, Vixen,' said the snake. 'Another spring and yet you look just the same.'

Compliments from Adder were few and far between. Vixen was conscious of the unusual distinction. 'How nice to be greeted in such a charming way,' she said graciously. 'And how good to see you after all this time.'

Adder uncoiled himself and slid towards her. His thin body was blunt at the tail where some time ago he had lost about two centimetres of his length in a tussle with an enemy fox.

'The Reserve is alive with frogs, it seems,' he remarked with his infamous leer. 'I must try to work up an appetite and make the most of them.' His tongue flickered in and out as he tested the air.

'That won't be very difficult after your long fast, I should think.'

'Oh, my cold blood needs time to heat up properly,' he

answered. 'I'm always a bit sluggish at first.'

Vixen explained what had happened at the pond.

'Yes, I've heard rumours,' the snake drawled. 'There seem to be all kinds of strange stories about. Some monster or other on the prowl, I believe?'

'I think that's an exaggeration,' Vixen said. 'But there *is* a fierce creature roaming the Park. None of us feels safe. And the worst of it is – we don't know what this creature *looks* like.'

Fox, hearing Adder's voice, had emerged from the earth. 'Tawny Owl is keeping a lookout on his night travels,' he added, after he and Adder had exchanged greetings.

'Hm. Well, I've seen nothing,' the snake said. 'Except –'

The foxes waited but Adder seemed to have forgotten what he was going to say.

'Except what?' Fox prompted.

'Oh, it's of no importance,' Adder hissed. He had quickly decided that something he had detected might alarm them further. 'Have you seen Toad?' he asked to divert them.

'Oh yes. He steers clear of the pond too,' Vixen told him.

'Mmm. I hope I come across him,' Adder murmured. 'Well, I'm off to sun myself,' he added abruptly. 'Then I'll be ready for those frogs.'

He disappeared rather hurriedly and Fox and Vixen looked at each other with wry expressions.

'He doesn't change,' Vixen observed.

'No, he doesn't,' Fox concurred. 'And I wouldn't want him to. But he's keeping something from us. I know him.'

* * * * *

Adder *was* keeping something back. Before he would say more, he wanted his suspicions about what he had seen confirmed or allayed. Toad was the one to do that. So the snake went in search of him.

He had not been misleading the foxes about sunning himself. He needed the warmth from a long bask in the sun to get his muscles working properly in case there should be a bit of travelling for him to do. He found a patch of dead bracken which faced into the spring sunshine. The spot was dry and the ground felt quite warm. It was ideal for him. While he enjoyed his sun-bath Adder reflected that it was just the opposite of the sort of place Toad would be seeking. Toad liked dampness and shelter from the sun's rays, and preferred to move about after dark.

When Adder felt thoroughly warm and sufficiently lively, he moved off. He was still in the part of the Park originally colonized by the band of Farthing Wood animals, and so he hoped he might meet some old companions. As he rippled through the dry dead stalks of grass he saw an animal rise from the ground a few metres in front of him. It was Leveret who, in a typical attitude, was standing on hind legs to look about him. Adder hastened forward, calling in his rasping way. He knew that if Leveret bounded off there would be no hope of his catching him again. No animal in the Park could move so swiftly. Luckily Leveret detected the snake's movement and dropped on all fours to await him.

'I thought it must be you,' he said when Adder came up. 'Well, it's a sign Spring has really and truly arrived when you are seen moving about.'

'I'm looking for Toad,' Adder stated bluntly, without offering a greeting.

'Yes. I see.'

'Well, can you help me?'

'I hope so, yes. What's the problem?' Leveret asked. The snake's tongue flickered faster than ever, a sure sign of his exasperation. It was always the same with this maddening animal, he thought. Everything had to be said twice. 'Can you help me find Toad?' he hissed slowly and emphatically.

'If you wish it, Adder. Now where shall we begin?'

'Oh, don't bother!' said the snake angrily. 'Perhaps I'll manage better on my own.'

Leveret looked surprised. 'But I thought – ' he began.

'Look,' said Adder. 'I'm going towards the pond. If you see Toad tell him to meet me there. I need his advice.' He slid away in a bad humour. 'Mammals!' he muttered.

Leveret watched his departure. 'Funny he should be going *to* the pond when everyone else has been moving away from it,' he said to himself.

— 3 —
Footprints and Eyes

Adder took a roundabout route to the pond. Always one of the most secretive creatures in his movements, he now used extra care in view of the new air of uncertainty in the Reserve. It was a while before he reached the pond and his progress had been arrested twice on the way by two plump frogs who had presented to him irresistible reasons for delay. But once near the water's edge in the early dusk, Adder was still able to see the strange signs he had detected before. He settled himself down amongst the reeds and sedges for what might prove to be a long wait. The surface of the pond was undisturbed in the evening calm and no sound – not a single croak or chirp – arose from the vegetation clothing its banks.

Toad had soon been rounded up by Leveret. He was puzzled by Adder's message but, since he well knew that the snake was not prone to seek another's company without a definite purpose, he agreed to set off for the rendezvous. It was with some considerable misgiving that Toad found himself returning to the scene of so much recent agitation. He decided to run no risks – even though he suspected a small creature like himself might be beneath the notice of the mysterious fierce hunter. He covered most of the distance to the pond in daylight, but as soon as he got close to the danger area he hid himself in some thick moss to await darkness. Then, with the benefit of its screen, he continued rather more confidently. However, he was still wary, and he paused often to listen. He reached the pond without noticing any evidence of an unusual presence abroad that night.

Toad gave a muffled croak once or twice in the hope that only the waiting Adder would recognize it. The snake had expected him to arrive after dark and had remained alert, so the ploy worked.

'Well, you've taken a chance,' Toad said in a low voice as he pulled himself into the waterside screen from which Adder hissed his position.

'Only a slender one if there's no chance of discovery,' Adder observed wryly. 'I want you to look at something, Toad, I'm at a bit of a disadvantage.'

'What do you mean?'

'That patch of mud,' Adder indicated in front of them. 'What do you make of it?'

Toad looked where he was bidden. After a while he said, 'Nothing much. Unless you mean – oh!' a little croak of alarm escaped him involuntarily.

'You see them then?'

'Paw prints!'

'I thought as much,' hissed the snake. 'But, you

understand, Toad, someone who relies on my sort of locomotion can't claim to be an expert in such matters.'

'I take your point,' said Toad. 'But there can be no doubt. The frightening thing is – '

'I know – the size of them. I suppose they've been made by a mammal?'

'Oh yes. No frog or toad in existence could make marks like that.'

'I first saw them a day or so ago,' Adder said, 'and didn't pay much attention. It's only now I realize their significance.'

'Do the others know?'

'*I've* said nothing. I wasn't sure. Well, Toad, this will put their fur into a bristle.'

'I wonder if we should tell them? I mean, LOOK! What size must the creature be?'

'Big enough to kill a deer. No, we can't leave them in ignorance. They should be prepared.'

'Prepared for what, Adder? What can they do?'

'Nothing, I imagine,' the snake answered bluntly, 'except – keep their wits about them.'

Toad recalled the birds' mission. 'The animal might have been seen by now. Tawny Owl is combing the park.'

'This creature's too clever to be found by an owl,' Adder remarked with a hint of contempt. 'It's a master of concealment.'

The notion entered Toad's head that the Beast might be lying hidden nearby at that moment, and keeping them under observation. He became very nervous. 'I – I –think we shouldn't stay here,' he chattered. 'It might come back at any moment and – and – we know it's active at night. Let's separate.'

'I think we're safe enough,' Adder drawled affectedly,

'But all right, Toad. Thanks for your advice. My fears were well founded.'

Toad muttered something about seeing Adder again 'in the usual place' and hopped hurriedly away. The snake made up his mind to stay awhile in case he might be able to add some more evidence to the existing clues.

In the meantime Tawny Owl was on his second reconnaissance flight. He combed the park methodically, concentrating on the areas most fitted to an animal who wanted to hide itself. But, like the first, this second night of searching produced nothing. Before dawn, Tawny Owl flew wearily to a favourite perch in a beech copse. He was very tired indeed, but was pleased with the way he had carried out his mission. He felt he had left, as it were, no stone unturned. He settled his wings sleepily and, little by little, his big round eyes closed.

The Moon shone brightly over the countryside. White Deer Park shimmered in its glow. Once or twice the owl shifted his grip on the beech bough. It was a bright night, and each branch of the tree was picked out sharply in the moonlight. Tawny Owl dozed. But something – some influence or other – prevented him from sleeping properly, despite his tiredness. He opened one eye and, from his high perch, looked down towards the ground. What he saw nearly caused him to fall from the branch. A huge face, with eyes glinting in the moonlight like live coals, stared up at him.

Tawny Owl lost his grip, overbalanced, flapped his wings frantically and just saved himself from plunging downwards head first. He let out a screech and fought his way awkwardly up through the branches, at last gaining sufficient height to feel safe. He veered away from the copse and steadied himself as he recovered from his sudden shock. The Beast!

As Tawny Owl calmed down he wondered if any other creature had seen his frightened reaction. He looked all round to see if he was watched and then alighted elsewhere, far enough away from his first spot to be comfortable. Now he wondered if he had imagined what he'd seen. It was so sudden – had he been dreaming? He did not think so, but he knew he ought to go back for a second look. After all, he was quite safe in the air. He thought about it for a while, trying to find valid reasons for not going back. But he could not think of any.

'Still. It's probably moved by now. Not much point,' he told himself unconvincingly. Then he thought of his friends. He owed it to them to make a proper report. He hesitated. Tawny Owl was not lacking in courage, but he really had had a bad fright. The Beast had been so close! At last he stiffened his resolve and took to the air once more, flying on a circular course which eventually brought him back to the borders of the beech copse. He fluttered to and fro uncertainly. Actually to enter the little wood again was extraordinarily difficult.

When he finally did fly in, he went cautiously from one tree to another, stopping each time before moving on. When the tree from which he had seen the Beast came into view, of course there was no sign of any animal, large or small, in its branches. A feeling of great relief flooded over the owl and now he flew right up to the tree for a closer look. Nothing!

'I shouldn't have delayed,' he muttered. 'It was wrong of me. Two great eyes – *that's* not much to go on. Now I suppose the thing's got well away from this place.' He flew about the copse, examining everything that might yield a clue. But there were no clues, not even footprints,

for last year's dry leaves were still thick on the ground.
And not the slightest rustle disturbed them.

Tawny Owl left the copse and directed his flight
towards Fox's earth. He began to feel quite proud of his
news. He, alone of all the Park's inhabitants, had had a
glimpse of the stranger who had come to dominate their
lives. It made him very important.

Day broke as he arrived. He called to Fox and Vixen
peremptorily. Already his mind was beginning to
exaggerate the little he had seen. There were stirrings in
the foxes' den. Vixen peered out.

'Oh, hallo, Owl,' she murmured and went promptly
back inside again.

'Wait!' cried the bird. 'I've news that – '

But Vixen was not listening. Tawny Owl could hear
voices inside the earth. He hooted with frustration. He
was bursting to tell them of his experience. Then Fox
emerged on his own.

'Have you had any luck, Owl?' he asked nonchalantly.

'Luck!' spluttered the bird. 'I – I – I've SEEN it!'

Fox looked at him sharply. 'The Beast? The hunter,
you mean?'

'Yes, yes. I came to tell you. I was in a tree and – and it
was *enormous*.'

'Did it attack you?'

'No. Oh-ho, no. I was too quick for that,' Tawny Owl
boasted. 'I was asleep, you see, Fox. I awoke and – there it
was.'

'You were asleep? Oh, I understand. And what did the
creature look like?'

The suspicion in Fox's voice was unmistakable and
Tawny Owl noticed it at once. Did he think he had
imagined it? Well!

'If that's your attitude,' he said resentfully, 'why should

I continue the story?'

'Now don't get in one of your huffs,' Fox pleaded. 'But sleep's a funny thing. We can all – '

'*All* doesn't come into it,' Owl interrupted haughtily. 'I alone have seen this thing. No one else was around. I was merely dozing after tiring myself out looking for the creature. I tell you I looked down and saw a massive head with gleaming eyes just below me. It was watching me! Do you think I invented it?'

'No, of course not,' Fox assured him. 'But – what was the rest of it like?'

'Ah well,' Owl mumbled, 'now you're asking. I wasn't able to see the *rest*.'

Vixen joined them. 'I overheard most of it,' she said. 'There's to be a meeting in the Hollow. Why doesn't Tawny Owl tell *everyone* about it then?' She was addressing Fox.

'A wise idea. It's tomorrow at dusk, Owl. Friendly and Charmer will come, and Weasel and Badger. And Whistler, of course. Perhaps he might have seen something too.'

'I doubt it,' Tawny Owl remarked jealously. 'The Beast doesn't reveal itself in the daylight.'

The Hollow was the traditional meeting place of the Farthing Wood community. It had been their first resting point on their arrival in the Park after their months' long journey. They had returned to it ever since when important matters were to be discussed, as a place of significance to them all.

The party assembled as darkness began to fall. Leveret and Squirrel were among the numbers. Toad arrived last, unwittingly bringing news to corroborate Tawny Owl's statement.

When Owl finished giving his description, which by

now he had embellished with all sorts of additional dramatic references, Toad croaked out what he and Adder had seen.

'I can vouch for the truth of Owl's remarks about size,' he added afterwards. 'The prints we saw could only have been made by a monster. Your feet, Fox, would have fitted into one corner!'

There was a silence and some of the animals looked at each other in consternation. Tawny Owl felt that his experiences were not getting the attention they deserved.

'Pooh,' he said, struggling to find words to bring his own experience back into the limelight, 'what are marks in the mud compared to a sight of the entire beast?'

Fox and Vixen looked at each other with wry amusement at the bird's childishness. But Toad wished Adder had been there to supply one of his caustic retorts. Owl could be very trying and silly at times. He had already admitted that he had seen only the head of the Beast clearly.

Badger asked if the prints had been like a cat's.

'Neither Adder nor I are qualified to tell you that,' Toad told him.

Badger turned to Tawny Owl. 'What about the head? Did it resemble a cat's?'

'Not in the least,' the bird answered immediately, without thinking about it. 'I told you you were on the wrong track.'

'But what other creature can climb a tree?' Badger persisted. 'Apart from our friend Squirrel.'

'None I know about,' Squirrel remarked.

The young foxes, Friendly and Charmer, were becoming impatient with the obtuseness of the ageing comrades.

'What does it signify whether it's a cat, a dog, a – a –

horse or a giant rat?' cried Charmer exasperatedly. 'It hunts. It kills. And it's very dangerous. Surely all that matters is what we can do to protect ourselves?'

Her brother Friendly supported her. 'Charmer's quite right,' he agreed. 'Whatever it is, we've got to think of a way to get it out of the Park.'

'But that's impossible,' Leveret said nervously, 'if we never know where it is.'

'We can track it,' Friendly declared. 'We foxes. It must have a scent.'

His father intervened. 'You're getting carried away, Friendly,' he said. 'Even if the scent could be picked up and then followed – which I doubt – what would the object be? What would you do if you came up against the creature?'

'Er – well, I – er – *we*, that is, would, I suppose – ' Friendly stopped in embarrassment. What *would* they do?

'You see, you haven't thought it through, have you?'

'All right, Father. But we must do *something*, mustn't we? Otherwise we could face extinction.'

'I only know what we mustn't do,' Fox returned, 'and that is confront it. This is a cunning, powerful animal quite beyond our experience. We're not dealing this time with rivals of our own kind.'

Now the attention of all the animals was fixed firmly on their old leader. Fox was the one to whom they had always turned when in trouble or danger. They respected him and trusted him. He had never yet failed to find a solution. They waited for him to go on. But the words of wisdom they expected to hear were not forthcoming.

'I'm afraid I've nothing to add to that,' he said finally.

The animals looked crestfallen.

'We have to defend our home – don't we?' Friendly whispered uncertainly.

'We can't,' said his father. 'I told you – it's beyond us.'

The little group exchanged glances unhappily. This defeatist Fox was unknown to them. They depended on him so much and he had never let them down before. Fox knew what they were thinking.

'I'm no longer a young animal,' he told them. 'We've all grown older. We can't indulge in the sort of escapades we used to do in the old days. We're no match for this Beast.'

'It's true,' sighed Badger. 'It's as much as I can do to get myself out of my set to feed sometimes.'

The young animals – Friendly, Charmer and Leveret – felt like intruders into an assembly of veterans. Friendly began to realize his father was, as always, trying to be realistic about their abilities. Perhaps it was time for the younger generation to take up the fight. But Fox was speaking again.

'To be blunt,' he said, 'there are some animals more at risk in the Reserve than others. Rabbits and, I'm afraid, hares, too, are the most vulnerable, as well as the smaller game such as mice, frogs and so forth. Foxes and badgers and snakes are not generally hunted for food. Birds, of course, have the perfect escape mechanism. So what I'm saying is that most of us are safe if we ensure that we don't antagonize the Beast.'

'That's a lot of comfort for me,' Leveret said morosely.

'I'm certain Fox didn't mean we'd turn our backs on you,' Vixen reassured him. 'The Oath of Mutual Protection still survives.'

'Of course,' said Fox. 'All of us are available to help another animal who gets into danger. But that's rather different from setting out to court it.' He looked meaningfully at Friendly.

Friendly said nothing, but he was eager for the meeting to break up. After what his father had said about foxes not being so much at risk, he had started to formulate some ambitious plans of his own.

— 4 —

A Waiting Game

The animals did not stay together much longer. The meeting had been inconclusive and the only message to come out of it was that they each needed to take extra precautions for as long as the Beast chose to make White Deer Park its hunting ground.

After Tawny Owl's fright no more was seen or heard of the stranger. Adder had seen nothing more, although he had waited for a long time at the pool's edge. This state of affairs continued for quite a while, and once again the Park's population returned to its main concern – the business of raising families. Even the Edible Frogs forgot their alarm and, in dribs and drabs, returned to the water.

Friendly had been down to the Pond in the meantime to see the reported footprints for himself, and to use his nose in the hope of finding a scent. But the stranger had moved on. The fox could find nothing useful and the mud where the stranger had left its pug marks now betrayed no hint of the unusual.

The animals started to hope again, although they still dared not believe that they were to be left in peace.

Then the Beast announced its presence with an emphasis that ruled out all their hopes. An old and infirm member of the deer herd that roamed the Park was killed. Its remains – and they were scanty – were found some time afterwards, lying under a screen of budding elm scrub. It chanced to be Friendly who came across them. He was shocked at the discovery but, in a strange way, excited too. For it meant that the heroic plans he had laid might still be adopted. At first he told no one about the evidence except his contemporaries. These younger foxes and their descendants formed quite a large group, all of whom were related to each other through the blood of their common ancestor, the Farthing Wood Fox. Whilst the females amongst them were occupied at the moment with their new offspring, the males had time to gather and listen to Friendly's news. The older animals were kept in ignorance for the time being.

'There was no mistaking the odour all round the carcass,' Friendly told them. 'It was a sharp, thin smell – quite detectable above the smell of the rotten meat. And it was an animal smell I've never picked up before in this Reserve!' He brought the last words out with an air of triumph.

'Did you try to trace it?' asked one of his own male progeny, who was now entering his second season.

'Yes, Pace. I followed it for a way back. Then the trail

lost its scent. But, between us, we should be able to pick it up somewhere else.'

'Then what would we do?' asked a nephew, one of his dead brother Bold's cubs.

'I want to trace it back to its lair,' Friendly explained. 'Once we've found that, we can choose our time to assemble together and corner the Beast. We'll make it understand it's not wanted around here. It can't fight all of us, however big it is.'

The other foxes were quiet. Friendly allowed them a while for his words to sink in. Some of them did not appear to be very comfortable with this plan. Others, the more adventurous among them, were enthralled at the possibility of routing such a remarkable predator.

'When would we begin this tracking down?' one asked.

'We'll let the Beast make the first move,' Friendly answered. 'Let it show itself. If it's too clever to allow itself to be seen, let it reveal its whereabouts by its activity. That carcass was an old kill. What we want to find is a fresh one. Then *that* would be our starting point.'

The foxes dispersed, most of them enthusiastic about the venture. The days passed. It seemed as if the stranger had an inkling of the plan, for no carcass was found. The Beast was taking great pains not to advertise itself.

There had been births in the White Deer herd, just as there had been births amongst all the other species that inhabited the Park. The stranger, having tasted deer flesh, was particularly interested in the new arrivals born to the herd. These babies promised an even more succulent meal than the first victim. So it had been stalking the deer in its silent way, waiting for the right moment to strike.

The moment arrived. The opportunity was taken. In the darkness the fawn's mother knew little about her loss.

The stealth, the swiftness of the stranger worked with a sweet harmony. It was a harmony that was also ruthless. The fawn was taken, carried off and devoured with a quietness that was bewildering. The tenderness of the hapless young deer enabled its killer to leave very little evidence in the way of remains. So it was easily overlooked by the foxes who were searching for clues while they hunted for themselves and their mates.

Friendly was baffled. He had expected the Beast would have given a hint of its hideout by this time. Now the animals were back to wondering if it was still around.

But now the Reserve Warden began to suspect that something was amiss. He was the last to become aware of the existence of a fierce killer in the vicinity. He knew how many births had taken place that season in the deer herd, and when he discovered the loss of one and, later, a second, he became suspicious. There was no sign of their bodies. So their deaths were not from natural causes. When on his rounds he discovered the rotting remains of the old animal that had first fallen prey to the Beast he knew at once a killer was hunting his deer. His first conclusion was that it was a dog, and he was well aware that such an animal, having once killed deer, will return again and again to the attack.

From that time on, the Warden kept a careful watch on the herd, making regular evening and early morning circuits near the deer's position. He saw and heard nothing at all. This puzzled him because he knew that a dog is not the most silent of animals, and he was an experienced and careful observer. What he did not know was that he had become watched: the killer the watcher.

So long as the Warden continued his daily rounds, the killer wisely contented itself with smaller game. But it had inexhaustible patience, and it knew that eventually there would be another opportunity to eat raw venison. The Warden had patience too. He expected the creature to strike again, and that this lull was a temporary one. He was quite sure it was still close by and he waited for its return. He carried a gun while on his rounds, since he had the authority to use it if necessary to ensure the protection of the rare white deer. And so a waiting game developed that was played by both sides.

Naturally the other animals were also interested in the frequent appearance of the Warden. They realized that human endeavour was now ranged against the intruder and the older ones were comforted. Friendly and the more daring young foxes had mixed feelings. They were heartened by the man's presence, but really they wished to have the glory of defeating this unknown enemy all to themselves.

Fox and Vixen had gone one day, as they sometimes did, to talk to the Great Stag, the leader of the deer herd. Like them, he had suffered the changes wrought by Time. It was a matter for speculation how long he would continue to lead his kind. By now Fox had heard of the deer losses.

'Can you add anything to the little we know of the killer?' he asked.

'I only know of its speed and its strength,' the Stag answered him. 'It's approach was unnoticed and its retreat unmarked.'

'What *can* we be up against?'

'An extremely efficient predator,' observed the Stag. 'Certainly one to worry our human friend as well as ourselves.'

'I have a sneaking feeling,' Fox declared, 'that he will meet with the same lack of success.'

'I can't comment on that,' was the reply. 'He has his

methods, I believe. But we must certainly hope other-wise. Because *we* have no defence against it.'

'None at all,' agreed Fox. 'I've already accepted that.'

'Oh, it won't be any concern to you,' the Stag went on. 'I think it unlikely it will show any interest in foxes.'

'We're only worried about some of our young friends being foolhardy,' Vixen told him. 'I'm sure Friendly sees himself as a sort of successor to Fox. He has a lot of confidence and courage.'

'Well, it must be in his blood, I suppose,' commented the Stag. 'But it would be a foolish enterprise, I fear, to attempt to tussle with this supreme hunter.'

'Yes. I prefer to respect it from a distance,' said Fox.

'And hope that before we're all much older it'll choose to go away,' Vixen added.

'I wouldn't hold out a lot of hope for that,' the Stag returned. 'The creature has had no opposition so far. I feel that, as long as there is a deer herd here, it will choose to stay. That is, unless it is persuaded otherwise.'

'It's a sobering thought,' Fox said solemnly.

'My hinds are in a proper turmoil about it. Their nerves are all strung up. And I can offer them no assistance.'

'Not while the Beast remains hidden,' Fox acknowl-edged. 'But you stags are about the only animals in the Reserve who might successfully oppose it in a fight. Surely one day it's going to make a slip and be seen?'

'Don't count on it,' the Stag advised him.

The three talked more. Then, with the Warden once again coming into view, Fox and Vixen departed.

*****

Adder had returned to his home area after quitting the pondside, using the secluded route that was habitual to him. He liked to enjoy as much of the spring sunshine as he could, and he lay amongst the bracken very often, sleepily absorbing the sun's rays. The first new fern shoots were just pushing their heads above the surface and the pale green tightly-curled heads carried a promise of the fragrance that was to come in the summer. One day Adder was lying in this way, his red eyes glinting in the sunlight. He was thinking about his next meal but he was in no hurry to look for it. His reptilian stomach did not require to be filled with the mechanical regularity of a bird's or a mammal's. Because of his proximity to the stream that ran through the Park, he happened to be the first recipient of news brought by a very flustered Whistler.

It was early morning and the heron had been standing in the shallows in his usual sentry-like posture. As he watched for the rippling movement of a fish, out of the corner of his eye he saw an animal move slowly along the bank away from him. It was some twenty metres away and appeared to be looking for the best spot to descend for a drink. Whistler's immobility had kept him unobserved. He noted the animal was large, with sleek brown and black fur in blotches of colour which merged into stripes on its back. Its body had a powerful but streamlined appearance, with a long, thin, furry tail. It got down to the water's edge and, leaning on its front legs, lapped thirstily. As it drank, it maintained a watchful eye on its surroundings. It paused two or three times to look about. When it was satisfied it raised itself, shook one front paw in a kind of fastidiousness, and moved away with an unhurried, loose and undulating motion. Whistler was impressed by the creature's graceful movement. It looked round once more and he caught just a glimpse of a round whiskered face with two green eyes, and small ears and nose.

Whistler had held himself quite still during this entire episode. But now he hastened to fly off. He flapped his long wings and, with his stilt-like legs trailing beneath, he gained height and turned in the direction of his friends. A few seconds later he spied Adder sunbathing. He dropped down briefly to tell him what he had seen.

'What do you think it was?' he asked the snake.

'Oh, the creature we've all been looking for,' Adder answered nonchalantly, without even shifting his position. 'No question about it.'

'I wondered the same myself,' Whistler replied. 'I must go and spread the word.' He gave a farewell 'krornk' and flew away.

Adder's feigned lack of interest turned into action as soon as the heron was gone. He slid furtively from his couch in the bracken and made for the stream side. There would be footprints by the water and he wanted to compare them. He went along the bank and his eyes soon picked out the place where the animal had drunk. Yes, there were the marks! He examined them for a while to make quite sure.

'Just as I thought,' he lisped to himself. 'Identical.'

Now his curiosity was aroused. He wanted to see the creature for himself. He debated whether it was safe to follow in its wake along the bank. There was very little cover at that spot and he wanted to remain undetected. Only in that way could he hope to have a chance of surprising the stranger. He slithered hastily into the nearest patch of vegetation. As he lay hidden his mind began to concentrate itself on a grand scheme.

Some seasons ago, Adder had been the chief victor in a battle that the Farthing Wood animals had fought against some foxes. These had resented the animals establishing a new home for themselves in the Reserve. The snake had a weapon more telling than any of his friends possessed – the weapon of poison. He had used it before to rid them of a dangerous enemy. Now he began to entertain thoughts of doing so again – and with much more purpose. For the stranger who had come to dominate their lives was more powerful and dangerous than any fox. And, as long as it lived amongst them, it was a potential enemy of every animal in the Park. Adder had no way of knowing if his poison was sufficiently potent to immobilize such a big hunter. So there was only one way of finding out.

The snake glided through the plant stems, intent on his secret pursuit. Surprise was everything. There was a patch of bare ground between the clumps of vegetation he needed to cross. But, once across it, the cover was thick and tangled again. He slid into the open. All was quiet. His head was about to enter the next mass of growth when the breath was driven from his body. A heavy weight came down in the centre of his back along his vertebrae. He was pressed against the hard ground so tightly that we was unable even to wriggle his tail. Adder was securely pinioned.

—5—
Strangers

Whistler sped on, his great steel-grey wings beating rhythmically. He began to call as he neared Fox and Vixen's earth.

'News! News! Sensational news!'

He made such a noise, and the noise was so unexpected from the normally dignified heron, that animals and birds came out of their burrows and holes and boughs, or stopped what they were doing, to look up at him. He hastened to land.

Fox and Vixen were all agog and an indignant and sleepy Tawny Owl flew to a nearby perch to hear what all the unwarranted (in his opinion) commotion was about.

'The Beast is seen!' Whistler cried by way of a preliminary. 'Drinking, as boldly and openly as you like, from the stream.'

More animals and birds were gathering to listen. There was a chorus of demands to know what it was like, in voices of many varied pitches and registers. The heron waited for the hubbub to die down. He was familiar with the ginger cat belonging to the Warden and so this was the obvious comparison to make.

'It was like,' he told them, and at once there was a hushed silence, 'a much larger version of the cat our Badger got to know so well.'

Tawny Owl blinked his great eyes in disbelief.

'The colouring was quite different,' Whistler added. 'But there was the same litheness of movement, the same suppleness, the same silent gait.'

The owl prepared himself to give a sharp retort if Badger should start saying 'I told you so.' He looked around, but Badger was not in the throng. Owl was glad – but felt he would have to defend his own argument sooner or later.

'Where did the creature come from?' Fox wanted to know.

'I didn't observe its approach,' replied Whistler. 'It was already on the bank when I first saw it. Then it drank and made off towards the nearest cover – thankfully in a direction away from this part of the Park.'

Friendly had been listening eagerly. He knew where Whistler preferred to fish and now at last he had the evidence that he needed. He did not wait to hear any more but ran off at once to round up his confederates.

'So we're dealing with a large, powerful cat,' Fox summed up. 'Well, it could be worse. But what kind of cat can it be? Certainly not a human's pet. It's something none of us have ever seen or heard about before.'

'Excuse me,' Tawny Owl interrupted in his pompous way. 'Aren't you jumping to conclusions, Fox? How do we know this is the animal that has been doing the killing?'

There was a pause while his words were considered. Tawny Owl felt he had produced an effect and he was much gratified.

'We don't *know*,' admitted Fox. 'But everything points to it.'

'Adder was quite clear about it as soon as I told him,' Whistler remarked.

'Adder?' Owl scoffed. 'Adder? What would *he* know about it?'

'Its very size, as Whistler describes it, must be a sufficient clue.' Squirrel said. 'And it's an animal that's quite new to us.'

'Just how big *was* it, Whistler?' Tawny Owl demanded, enjoying his position as the cautious dissenter.

The heron tried to give as vivid an impression as he could of the powerful body, the shape of the head – even the eyes. 'They had a cold gleam in them,' he said, 'just as you would expect to see in the eyes of a calculating, ruthless killer.'

'Stuff and nonsense,' Tawny Owl returned. 'There's a lot of your imagination gone into that description, Whistler. They don't sound a bit like the eyes *I* saw in my tree. It's certainly not the same beast.'

Tawny Owl had caused quite a stir, which is what he had intended. Were there *two* powerful strange animals roaming the Park? The animals started chattering all at once in a nervous way so that it was quite impossible for Whistler to make himself heard. Fox tried to think constructively, but that was impossible too.

Vixen said to him quietly, 'At least none of us is immediately threatened. We've got the time to think more about it, but now's not the right moment.'

'Just so,' agreed Fox, and they indicated to the heron that they were returning to their den.

'Someone should tell Badger your news,' Weasel said to Whistler. 'No one should be kept in the dark.' He ran off towards Badger's set.

Leveret mentioned that Toad was not present, but Whistler thought it likely that he might be found near the stream.

'And that takes care of everyone,' he summarized. He had no more to add and flew back to his usual haunt, though with the necessary circumspection.

Tawny Owl found himself surrounded by a miscellany of birds who bombarded him with questions about his experience with the Beast. He did not much relish this position, now that his close companions had gone on their way. It was daytime, he was sleepy, and he was never very comfortable in the company of a host of songbirds who sometimes chose to mock him during his periods of inaction in the daylight. Whilst he was trying in vain to disentangle himself, Weasel arrived at the entrance to Badger's home.

The first thing he noticed as he went in was the sound of voices. Badger lived alone and Weasel wondered to whom he was talking.

A voice, very like poor Mole's, was distinguishable. Weasel paused some way down the tunnel to listen to the conversation.

'You don't know how happy you've made me,' next came the gruff sound of Badger's voice. 'I really had given you up for lost.'

'But, you see, Badger, you're getting muddled,' said the Mole-like voice.

'Muddled?' Badger repeated. 'Oh yes, at my age – I

suppose you're right. I expect I do get muddled. But what does all that matter? What's important to me is that my dear old friend has come back. I *have* been rather lonely, Mole. Now we can have our cosy little talks again just like we always did. And I – '

'No, no,' the shriller voice interrupted. 'I'm not who you think. Oh dear. What can I say?'

Weasel detected a tone of helplessness in this voice and he began to put two and two together. He went on towards Badger's sleeping chamber. It was very dark deep inside the set so he could not see either of the other animals. He hurriedly announced himself.

'Oh! Weasel,' said Badger. 'What brings you here?' He did not wait for an answer but went on immediately with unmistakable excitement: 'This is a wonderful moment. Mole has returned! We've just been — '

A wail from the animal cut him short. It was a sound Mole had never been heard to make in *his* life. 'I am a mole,' said the unhappy creature. 'But not the one you want. *He* was my father!'

Weasel was glad he could not see Badger's reaction. He would have found it too distressing.

'I – I blundered into your set through one of the passages. I know my father used to use these tunnels,' the young mole explained. 'I can be company for you, and willingly, if you wish it. But I can't be the mole you want – only myself!'

Weasel thought he had never been witness to such a pathetic encounter before and he heartily wished he was elsewhere. He tried to divert the conversation.

'I've come to tell you, Badger,' he said awkwardly, 'about a discovery. Whistler has seen a great cat, and we think it must be the Beast.'

There was a deep silence. Weasel wondered if he was understood. Then Badger said, 'Cat? A great cat? Well, I wonder what we should do about it. What do you think, Mole?'

Weasel stared into the darkness in disbelief. Was Badger's mind wandering? He seemed not to have grasped what the little animal had told him. And this time the young mole remained quiet. Perhaps he had decided it was futile to make a further denial. Or perhaps he was too stunned to speak.

'You suggested, didn't you, Badger, that the stranger seemed to have feline characteristics?' Weasel prompted.

'What? Oh, oh yes, Weasel,' Badger murmured. 'I did. I recall it. But I don't think I can do anything for you, you know. I'm really getting very feeble now . . . .'

'No one expects you to do anything,' Weasel assured him. 'I merely brought you the news. It helps to know what we're up against.'

Suddenly Badger's mind seemed to have a moment of startling clarity. He said, much more briskly, 'No doubt Tawny Owl has refuted the notion of a cat, straight away?'

Weasel was impressed. 'Well, yes, he did, in a way. How did you guess?'

'Oh, Weasel,' Badger chuckled, 'don't you think I know our Owl after all this time?'

Badger's shrewdness did not tally with his previous confusion. Weasel began to realize that the old creature had wanted to believe Mole had returned and was rejecting the truth. He had shut out the idea that Mole was gone and was going to use his youngster as a substitute.

'Well, where's the harm in it, if it gives him comfort?' Weasel said to himself. He had an idea. He whispered to the young mole whose velvety fur his whiskers had located nearby, 'Go along to the outer tunnel. I'll join you there.'

When Weasel was sure they were alone he said to Badger, 'I haven't any more to tell you for the present. I'm sorry you've been lonely. We can't expect you to go visiting so much now, so we must come to you. And I, for one, promise to do so.'

'Thank you, Weasel. How very kind,' said Badger joyfully. He seemed to be quite moved. 'Do, please. I should enjoy it.'

They bade each other farewell and Weasel made haste to find the perplexed young animal who had, quite unintentionally, got himself into such a pickle.

'Come to the set entrance,' he said to him.

The youngster obliged.

Now Weasel was a last able to see him properly. When he had a good look he was astonished to note just how much the young mole resembled his father. 'What do they call you?' he asked him.

'My father used to call me Mossy,' was the answer. 'I'm not quite sure why, unless it had something to do with the texture of my coat.'

'Well, listen – er – Mossy,' Weasel said. 'From now on you can allow yourself to be called just plain Mole. It's for the old badger's sake, of course. He won't know the difference, as you must already be well aware. It'll mean such a lot to him, and what does it matter? Will you mind?'

'Er – well, no, I suppose not. But won't it be confusing?'

'Not at all,' Weasel answered. 'I can soon explain the situation to the others. Thank you, my young friend. And, by the way, do drop in to Badger's set now and then. I know you offered.'

'I will. I meant what I said, Weasel. I feel sorry for him and he's always been such a kindly creature.'

'Good. Well, I'll leave you. Oh, and remember, if he

starts to talk about 'The Old Days' – which you know nothing about – just agree with him. That's all he expects, really.'

Mossy watched Weasel's pencil-slim body make its retreat and sighed. 'Ah well,' he murmured, 'I suppose it's not much to ask.'

Tawny Owl had managed to disengage himself from the attentions of the other birds and was now trying to doze, away from interference, in a hollow tree. But since all of his friends knew this favourite place, the exasperated owl was disturbed again by Weasel.

'I just dropped in to tell you I've seen Badger,' Weasel explained.

Much irritated, Tawny Owl snapped, 'Is that all you've woken me up for? How kind of you!'

'No, no, there's something you should know. I'm passing the message to everyone.' He went on to describe the scene in Badger's set involving Mole's offspring.

'Humph! So his mind's addled,' was Owl's comment on Badger. 'I might have known – the way he kept on about the strange animal being like a cat!'

Weasel refrained from pointing out that it looked as if Badger was correct in that. He contented himself with saying, 'I don't think his mind's addled at all. He's playing a sort of game with this young mole and I think we all ought to play along with him.'

'Pooh!' scoffed Tawny Owl. 'I'm past playing games. Badger ought to see sense. At his age too!'

'That's just it, Owl, "at his age". He's very old. I really don't think we'll have him around much longer. So why can't we humour him? I'm sure Fox and Vixen won't mind.'

'Oh, I can't be bothered with all that nonsense,' said Tawny Owl. 'Haven't we got more important things to think about?' He ruffled his feathers, re-settled his wings and closed both his eyes in a very determined sort of way. Weasel knew that he was dismissed.

As he had expected, Fox and Vixen and, indeed, all of his other friends whom Weasel managed to find, were agreeable to keeping up the pretence for Badger's sake. They were upset by the idea of Badger being in his dotage, and they tried to push to the backs of their minds the thought that it might not be long before they were without him.

Weasel's message did not get to Adder or Toad that day. But Whistler found Toad in the early evening and quickly told him of his important news, as well as that of Badger.

'And I have some news for *you*,' Toad said, 'while we're on the subject of the Beast. One of the frogs told me and *he* had been told by another and that one by another and so on. You know how fast news can travel through the Reserve. The upshot is that, despite the Warden's patrols, another deer has been killed.'

—6—

The Trail of the Beast

Adder could see nothing of his attacker. He was unable to turn to look behind, and the pressure was so great on his body that he thought his bones might break. There were no animals in the Park who ate snake and so Adder was in no doubt that he was trapped either by a human foot, or, more likely, by the very creature he had intended himself to surprise. There was a momentary easing of the pressure and Adder at once tried to turn. As soon as he moved, a huge paw swung round and patted at his head. Luckily for him the claws were retracted.

For the first time in his life Adder was really scared. He was scared in a way that he would not have been if the beast who was attacking him had been one he understood – such as a fox or a hawk. Fear of the unknown coursed through his sluggish blood. He felt he had no hope of escape. Then, abruptly, the great weight bearing down on his back was removed.

For a moment Adder's fear kept him frozen into immobility. He awaited the great blow that would crush the life out of him. But his paralysis lasted only a moment. Then he squirmed away painfully, in a desperate bid to reach the patch of vegetation. He was not permitted to. The paw descended again and knocked him back. The Beast was toying with him.

Adder kept moving – first this way, then that. Each time he was knocked back into place. Once a blow lifted him up into the air. He landed awkwardly. Pain racked his body but still he strove to get away. The Beast prodded him, tapped him and, finally, he felt its claws sear through his skin. He imagined he was going to be killed slowly in a form of torture, just as a cat will torment a bird or a mouse before the final kill. He wriggled in vain, like a creature in its death throes. Then a particularly heavy blow hooked him up high above the ground, over the vegetation, and suddenly Adder's scaly coils landed with a plop in the shallow part of the stream.

Like all snakes he was a good swimmer and, before he quite knew where he was, he instinctively rippled away into the deeper water. Only his head protruded above the surface. He looked back towards the bank and saw his assailant for the first time quite clearly. The Beast was staring out at the stream in an attempt to discover where its plaything had gone. Adder kept himself well hidden. After a while the Beast got bored and slowly padded away.

For a long time the snake dared not approach dry land,

although the water felt as cold as ice. He had to keep moving to avoid sinking to the bottom, but he merely swam through a cluster of weeds and then back again, until he was convinced the Beast would not return.

He made his way to the bank and slowly, painfully, drew his battered body into a cluster of rushes and reed mace. Here he rested and nursed his wounds. He was scratched, bruised and some of his scales were torn, but his bones were sound and for that Adder was profoundly grateful. All his grandiose ideas of performing the heroic act of ridding White Deer Park of this menace, seemed now to him piffling and nonsensical. A paltry creature like him trying to meddle with this great hunter from an unknown world! Why, he was no more than a worm who afforded a minute or two's distraction as a toy for such a powerful beast. Any animals who had made their homes in the Park had about as much chance of diverting it from its intentions as of learning how to walk on two legs. Adder would have chuckled at the absurdity of such a notion if he had been capable of it.

When he had recovered a little he moved carefully away from the stream, always keeping himself well screened, and slid with the utmost caution towards that quarter of the Reserve where his friends maintained their community. He had to make them understand about this Beast in no uncertain manner. But it was not until dusk that he approached close.

Toad was the first to hear of Adder's horrible encounter. He was full of sympathy.

'Oh Adder,' he croaked, 'my old friend! What a pounding you have had. Do come and rest yourself a little. There's a clump of moss I frequent which is as soft as thistledown. I'm sure if you lie there a while – '

'I'm much obliged, Toad,' Adder interrupted, 'and I'll take you up on your offer later. But I really feel Fox, at least, should know what we have to contend with.'

'I think he's aware of it already,' Toad returned.

'No. How could he be? He hasn't seen the creature. I tell you, Toad, we're all at its mercy. We're minnows by comparison.'

'Yes. Even the deer are suffering. Another one has been pulled down. I've just been telling Whistler. So despite the Warden's efforts – '

'Oh, the Warden!' hissed Adder. 'What can he do? Can he live amongst the deer herd? No. This hunter will take what it likes without hindrance. First it's at the pond, then it's by the stream or in a wood or choosing its prey in the open. It moves at will.'

'Is it the same creature?' Toad enquired.

'The same? What do you mean?'

'The same creature who caught you – did it make those footprints we saw?'

'My dear Toad, identical marks are all along the bank of the stream. That was how I was caught. I went to look.'

'It seems that Tawny Owl holds the view that there are two different beasts.'

Adder did not reply at once. Then he said in his driest lisp, 'If there are two, then our days are truly numbered. But I don't believe it. And now I must carry my warning.'

The snake's body was aching all over but he moved on. Fox's earth was empty. It was dark and, as usual, Fox and Vixen were on their evening quest for food. Their absence, however, at least gave Adder a chance of taking a proper rest. He awaited their return with patience.

As he lay, sleepily coiled up near the den entrance, another animal blundered into his path. There was an exclamation of surprise in a gruff, wheezy voice.

'It's only me, Badger,' Adder said evenly.

'Oh! So it is. I'm sorry. My sight was never very good and it seems to get worse. But I'm glad to see you. We don't often – '

'I'm glad to see *you*,' Adder butted in, 'because I'm bringing a warning.' He described his alarming tussle in dramatic terms.

'Goodness!' said Badger. 'You're lucky to be in one piece. But are you all right? Are you in pain at all? I can't see you very well . . . .'

'I shall survive,' Adder replied grimly. 'But I warn others – don't meddle with this creature!'

'Oh, I'm sure there is no question of it,' Badger said at once. 'That was Fox's advice before this happened. I doubt if anyone is contemplating such a thing.'

Adder said drily, 'It might surprise you to know that one was.'

'You?' cried Badger. 'But why? I mean, what could you have done?'

'That's immaterial now,' Adder drawled. 'But if *I* had the idea, another might too. That's why I'm here.'

Badger pondered this. He could not imagine any of the elders of the Farthing Wood community being so foolish. But he thought it would be tactless to say so, and, to change the subject, began to talk about the Warden and the recent deer killing.

Eventually Fox and Vixen appeared, and Adder told his story to them with his attendant warning.

'This is timely advice,' Fox said, 'because I already have a sneaking suspicion that something might be afoot. Vixen and I have seen no other foxes around this night, although we covered quite a lot of ground. Usually we come across at least one or two of the youngsters out roaming. I wonder if they are up to something?'

*****

Friendly had three young foxes in particular who looked up to him. There was his own son Pace, so called because of his speed; and there were two of his nephews. One was the son of Bold, known as Husky, who had his dead father's stout appearance. The other was Charmer's son, Rusty. Friendly's endearing qualities which had given him his name had attracted these youngsters and they were easily led by him. There were others, too, who had ties of one sort or another: Ranger, Charmer's mate; and a cousin of Ranger's, called Trip. Many of the vixens were fully occupied just then with their new litters, but Friendly had managed to gather together these five males – a substantial group – to join him on his expedition against the stranger who still threatened the peace of the entire Reserve.

He lost no time in leading them to the stream where the Beast had at last been seen in the open. None of these foxes knew anything of Adder's narrow escape, for that had happened while they were gathering.

Friendly soon noticed the Beast's spoor in the damp, soft ground at the edge of the stream. Working from there, he detected a scent and began to follow it along. The others ran behind. The youngest of them were both excited and frightened. Friendly had told them they were to track the stranger to its lair. He had not enlarged on what then was to be their purpose, but they were happy to be on an adventure and eager to prove themselves. Ranger and Trip brought up the rear of the party. They were about the same age as Friendly and of a cooler temperament.

The trail led through vegetation and then seemed to take a direction away from the water. The scent was fainter but Friendly was still certain of it, and it led them eventually into a wooded area.

'Now we must go very, very carefully,' he said. 'There's plenty of cover here and any scrub or undergrowth could be a hiding-place.'

A greenish light pervaded the enclosure. The young, newly-opened leaves made a thick screen which filtered the sun's rays. Last year's dead leaves and fallen twigs snapped and rustled underfoot, despite the animals' cautious movements. After a while Friendly lifted his head to listen, twitching his ears. He could find no unrecognized sound and bent his wet nose once more to the ground. He lost the scent and circled for a while before he picked it up again.

'Over here,' he called softly to the others, who had waited where they stood.

Friendly was moving slowly towards a mass of bramble which surrounded the base of an ancient hawthorn. Ranger had a sudden premonition.

'Take care!' he barked.

Friendly turned at the sharp sound and, as he did so, something stirred in front of him in the depths of the undergrowth. There was a muffled snarl and then the thing was gone, through some bolt-hole known only to itself, and with just the slightest disturbance of the low-lying foliage on the briars.

Friendly plunged after it, without stopping to think of the consequences. The other foxes hovered nervously, trying to peer in amongst the brambles. But they could see nothing. They could only hear their companion as he crashed through the undergrowth.

Now the youngsters turned to Ranger. 'What shall we do?' they asked. Pace said, 'Shouldn't we follow him? He's put himself in danger.'

'No. Stay together,' Ranger advised tensely. 'We're safer in a group and we might have to fight. We can't risk being picked off separately.'

'But what about Friendly?' asked Rusty.

Ranger did not answer.

The young foxes looked hesitantly from one to the other. They looked at Ranger and Trip who seemed uncertain of themselves. Without Friendly around, none of them had much confidence. The moments passed. A silence had fallen on the wood. The quietness seemed to them to be sinister.

'Sh – shall we wait a bit longer?' stammered Husky. It was obvious the way his mind was working.

'Yes. I think so,' Ranger answered, trying to sound calm. But their thoughts were all taking the same direction.

'I – er – don't see the point . . . .' Trip began, and then his voice petered out. He had caught a sound in the distance – a mere whisper, as of a brushed leaf. There was a soft swish of vegetation, nearer this time. The foxes' legs quivered. They were on the verge of scattering.

Then they heard Friendly's voice. 'It's no good – we missed him this time,' he called. They saw him approaching, but from another corner of the wood.

'There was just a glimpse,' he said as he came up. He was panting. 'A tail, I think.' He looked exhilarated. 'Anyway, we found its hideout – or one of them.'

'I don't think that's much help now,' Ranger said to him. 'Whatever was in there won't use it again, now it's known. The Beast is far too subtle for that.'

'*Was* it the Beast?' asked Pace in a whisper.

'Oh yes, I'm sure of it,' answered Friendly. He turned to Ranger. 'You're quite right, of course,' he said. 'No good looking here again. But the significant thing is – the creature ran! It didn't care to face all of us.'

The young foxes looked very pleased at this. They felt proud that Friendly had included them in the achievement, although they had not actually done anything definite.

'We can foil this beast,' Friendly continued confidently. 'We can drive it away from here.'

'Maybe we can,' said Ranger. 'But how do we ever get close to it? It's vanished again now, so I suppose we must start our search anew?'

Friendly considered for a moment. 'We could at least stay around this area for a while,' he said. 'It might not have gone far.'

The foxes stationed themselves at widely-spaced points so that they could cover quite a stretch of that part of the Park. They settled down for a long wait.

It was while they were waiting that the stranger killed its third deer. It was another fawn: only a few days old. The kill was sudden, silent and swift, just as before. Once again it seemed the Great Stag and all the adults of the herd were powerless to prevent it.

The meal was devoured in quite another corner of the Reserve and, by nightfall, the foxes themselves were feeling hungry. Ranger left his place and moved over to Friendly.

'I think we might as well call it a day,' he suggested.

'But it's the night when we should have the best chance,' Friendly replied. 'That's when this beast is most active.'

'Think of the youngsters,' said Ranger. 'Do they have the endurance? It could be a trial of nerves.'

'We shall be nearby – and Trip too,' returned Friendly. 'But perhaps I am expecting too much,' he added as an afterthought.

'I'm sure they must be famished,' Ranger remarked, 'if they feel anything like me.'

'Yes, very well. Let them refresh themselves,' said Friendly. 'But we'll wait on – shall we?'

Ranger looked glum, but his expression was hidden by

the dark. He kept his feelings out of his voice. 'Of course, if you think it will do any good.'

'It's worth a try,' answered Friendly. 'Will you tell the others then? And when they've fed they can come back. I have a feeling that, between us, we might be able to do something really worthwhile tonight.'

Trouble in Store

Fox and Vixen wondered what trouble Friendly and his followers could be getting themselves into. Then they discussed what, if there were to be trouble, *they* would be able to do about it. It did not take long for them to accept that there was nothing they – Fox and Vixen – *could* do. Friendly was no young cub to be reprimanded by seniors. He was a mature male into his third season who had strong ideas of his own and who, although he might listen politely to advice, would not necessarily act upon it. As for the younger foxes of a later generation, they were so remote in age from the elders that they might not even be prepared to listen.

'They must go their own way,' Vixen summed up.

'Yes,' said Badger who had remained with his old friends. 'Our day is done. All *I* hope for is sufficient peace and quiet to last me out.'

'I'm afraid we can't look forward to much of that at present, the way things are,' Fox said realistically. 'The Beast is still very much in evidence, as the latest deer killing shows. And Adder says it was done in daylight, so now there's a new dimension. The creature grows bolder. It seems to think nothing of stealing what it requires from under the nose of the Warden.'

'The problem does seem insoluble,' Badger agreed. 'But we know quite well humans are not fools. This brave hunter is likely to go one step too far.'

This notion comforted them all a little. Adder had left them to take advantage of Toad's proffered couch of moss. He had, so far, been the only surviving victim of an attack by the feared stranger. The others stayed talking a while, but Fox and Vixen were all on edge. They waited only for one of the younger foxes to put in an appearance. Eventually Badger went on his way. No fox came near.

Adder had barely made himself comfortable, after following Toad's directions, when he caught the vibrations of another creature moving along the ground nearby. His forked tongue flickered from his mouth as he tried to detect what sort of scent was given off. He was hoping for a tasty titbit in the shape of a frog, or maybe a shrew. His empty stomach felt like a cavern inside him. The leaves disturbed by the creature's progress crackled faintly. It was evident that it was something not very large. Adder was philosophical. Snails or large earthworms were all grist to the mill when you had not eaten for days.

The one thing he had not expected to come into view was another snake. But that was exactly what it was – and another adder, too. The snake came up quite close, slithering smoothly over the moss with an air of preoccupation. It did not speak to him.

Adder wondered if it meant to slide on past without appearing to notice him. For some reason, of which he was not quite sure, he felt indignant.

'I am alive,' he said sarcastically, 'not just part of the leaf litter.' Then he wondered why he had said it.

The other snake stopped and looked at him with the unwavering stare of their kind.

'Oh – yes. I see you are,' it replied phlegmatically. 'Have you been in a fight?'

'Well, I have. You're very observant.' Adder had not realized his scars were so obvious. Then he remembered his blunt tail. 'It's an old wound,' he added. 'It doesn't bother me.' He was a little surprised to discover that he was addressing a female.

'You're an old warrior, it seems,' returned the she-viper. 'There are scratches all over your body.'

Adder suddenly felt proud of his scars. For the life of him he did not know why. 'You're not often in this neck of the woods?' he ventured to enquire.

'Not very often. I've been looking for frogs. This is a good terrain for them when they're not in the water. But I was about to rest.'

'I'm doing the same myself,' said Adder. 'I can recommend this spot for comfort.' (What *was* he saying?)

'Well, since you recommend it, then,' said the female, 'I suppose I'd be a fool to ignore you.'

Adder did not know what to say next. He was quite unaccustomed to making pleasantries.

'There's been an abundance of frogs about this season,' the female went on. 'I've found them in all sorts of places.'

'Yes,' said Adder. 'And there's a reason for it.'

'A reason? Oh, I suppose you mean there was a glut of tadpoles last spring?'

'No, I don't mean that,' Adder hissed at her confidentially. 'It's a reason to do with a change of habitat.'

The other snake did not know what he was talking about and did not seem to be especially interested anyway. She made no reply.

Adder waited in vain. He was disappointed. He had been hoping to show off the depth of his knowledge. At length he said: 'You see, they took to the land at a time when they should have been in the water.' (He had an inkling this sounded rather foolish.)

'Really? Do tell me more,' came the toneless reply. It was obvious the she-viper was quite bored by the topic.

'You see, they were forced to leave the pond by a strange and powerful hunter.' Adder drew the words out slowly to heighten the dramatic effect.

'You mean the Big Cat? Oh yes, I know about that,' said the female. 'Have you only just heard the news? I should have thought every beast and bird in the Park would know by now.'

Adder was taken aback and, indeed, a little affronted. She had made him feel small and he did not think she was trying particularly hard to be polite.

'Er – yes,' he muttered. 'But how do *you* know about it being like a cat?'

'What a funny question,' she commented. 'Because I've seen it, of course!'

Her manner really was very abrupt, Adder decided. He did not know why he was bothering with her. Politeness was not something he normally cared very much about, one way or the other. He was preparing himself for one of his most sarcastic retorts when the female snake spoke again.

'I've just had a thought,' she hissed. 'Those scratches of yours. They couldn't be – '

'Yes!' Adder cried triumphantly. His attitude changed at once. 'I was mauled by the "Big Cat", as you call it.'

'I guessed as much,' she returned. 'You must have been very careless to have got in its way. It couldn't have been chasing you, because it doesn't feed off snakes!'

Adder had been mistaken in thinking his scars had impressed her. Now his anger began to kindle. Who was she to make comments about his carelessness?

'I'm afraid you're speaking from ignorance,' he said sourly. 'The stealth of this beast is more than enough to annul the most painstaking efforts at caution any other creature could make.'

The female snake looked at him for a few moments. She could tell she had annoyed him. 'Now don't get in a coil,' she said easily. She seemed to be preparing to rest, for she slithered away for a few centimetres. Adder heard her murmur to herself, 'Goodness, what a pedantic reply!'

His red eyes glared into the darkness. The mossy couch no longer seemed so soft and comfortable. He had not realized how offended he had been. He – the Farthing Wood Adder! What had *she* done to compare with his exploits? The more he thought, the more irritated he felt. In the end he could not bear to remain any longer in her company. Without another word he slid away, and it was not until he had put a fair distance between them, that he stopped again.

Before he quite sank into his usual nocturnal state of dormancy, Adder considered his reaction. *Why* had he been so irritated? What was this female to him that he should care so much as a fern-frond for her opinions? He was not sure he knew the answer. But he had half a mind, when daylight should arrive again, to return to Toad's clump of moss to see if she was still around – even if only to tell her what he thought of her!

The news of the deer killing was brought to Friendly by his young companions. Husky, Pace and Rusty had gone in search of food as had been suggested. They had kept close together to give themselves courage. Because of this they did not feel they had to restrict themselves in their range, and they wandered quite far. It was Husky who found the body. As usual, most of it had been consumed. The remainder was lying amongst some undergrowth, and there was no mistaking the freshness of the meat. The blood around it had hardly dried. Husky did not delay in bringing it to the attention of the other two.

'How could it have done that so quickly after escaping from us?' Pace asked rhetorically.

'Us?' Rusty echoed with a wry look.

'Well, Friendly, then . . . .'

'It moves as it pleases, doesn't it?' Husky said. 'It chooses its victim. It stalks it. And then it snatches it with the utmost ease.'

'I wish I had such confidence and such skill,' Pace remarked. 'I'd like to see the Beast in action. I can imagine the whole sequence – the smoothness, the stealth . . . .'

Husky was looking at the remains. 'Well, are we going to waste this?' he demanded of the others.

There was a silence. Then Rusty said, 'But we – we – daren't.'

'Why not?' Husky returned cockily. 'Can you see old "Stealth" around, or hear him?'

'No, but that's not to say he's not in the vicinity. How should *we* know?'

'We don't,' Husky declared. 'But I'm hungry – and there's more than one of *us*.'

'I – I don't think it would be wise,' Pace cautioned. 'The Beast might be planning to come back and finish this.' But as he looked at the meat and smelt again its freshness, he began to drool.

'Come on,' Husky urged him. 'We might not get another opportunity like this.' He bent and took a small piece of flesh from the carcass. 'You'll regret it if you don't,' he pronounced. 'Trust "Stealth" to choose himself the finest game.'

Pace did not need any more persuasion, and eventually Rusty too joined in the meal. It was an act of bravado, really, by these youngsters urging each other on. None of them were at ease as they ate. Their ears twitched to and fro constantly, trying to pick up the faintest of warning sounds. They chewed the meat stiff-legged, ready to dart away at the first moment. All the time their spines tingled and the hair on their backs rose slightly in a sort of awareness at the risk they were taking. But they were not interrupted and, when they had finished, they were all in agreement that they should return at once to the wood where Friendly and the older foxes awaited them.

They ran quickly, without any deviation from the route. They looked forward excitedly to Friendly's surprise when they would tell him of their audacity. As they loped along in high spirits, they were watched from a low branch of an oak by a pair of unblinking, gleaming eyes. Not one of them went unheeded. Not one of their actions was unperceived.

Friendly's reaction was not entirely as they had expected. He looked concerned at their news, and they thought they were about to be reproached for their daring. But he reminded himself how faithfully they had followed him and he had not the heart to issue a rebuke.

He even went so far as to remark that he liked their cheek.

Ranger, however, make them understand that he thought they had been very foolish. 'You don't know what trouble you might have stored up for yourselves,' he told them. 'If the Beast takes it into its head to teach you a lesson, don't come running to *me*.' He was ravenously hungry and the young foxes' foolhardiness only aggravated his general feeling of discomfort.

'You know you don't mean that, Ranger,' Friendly reasoned with him. 'We all stand together on this. We formed our group for a purpose and we can't back down now.'

'Well, there's no more to be done tonight,' Ranger asserted positively. 'We can't go off hunting now, we adults, and leave the juniors unattended. Not after what they've just told us. What do you think, Trip?'

'I agree with you,' said his cousin. 'There's always another day.'

'Of course there's another day,' said Friendly. 'But on another day we'd have to start from scratch again trying to pick up a trail. I still feel our best chance of success is *now*. I'm willing to ignore my stomach for the rest of the night if necessary.'

'Well, I'm not,' said Ranger bluntly. 'The situation's changed. We've lost the element of surprise. We might find that the Beast will decide to come looking for *us*.'

'Perfect!' was Friendly's reply. 'It would find it had made a grave mistake. How could it cope with the entire group of us?'

Trip decided the matter by siding with Ranger. 'It's too clever for that. Now let's go and feed. We can meet again tomorrow.'

Friendly saw he must succumb. 'So be it,' he said, trying to mask his exasperation. 'You youngsters must take us at dusk to this latest kill, and we'll begin to track it from there. We may find it easier next time, for we'll be following the taint of blood.'

—8—
New Measures

Toad returned to his mossy base later that night. He had fed well on slugs and insects, and he was in a good humour. He was keen to see if Adder had found the spot because he was feeling rather talkative. When he saw the mosaic coils of the snake at rest on his soft bed, he was delighted.

'Well, you've certainly made yourself comfortable,' Toad began, 'and – goodness! – it really looks as if your scratches are healing already!'

The she-viper raised her head and regarded the small amphibious animal who addressed her. Her eyes glared greedily, for she thought at first she was looking at a frog.

But when she realized it was a toad she lost interest. She knew how unpalatable toads were and, without saying a word, settled herself once more.

Toad was surprised and a little disappointed at the snake's reaction. But he knew how unpredictable Adder was. You could never be quite confident that he would be in a friendly mood. Then he remembered his recent experiences and wondered if Adder were in pain or feeling unwell.

'Are you all right, Adder?' Toad asked with real concern.

The snake looked up again. 'I'm perfectly well,' she answered smoothly, 'though I must confess I'm somewhat puzzled at your interest.'

Now Toad realized his mistake and, quite unconsciously, hopped a little further away. A strange snake was always a potential enemy. 'I – I took you for another,' he muttered and began at once to move off.

'I think I met him,' was the unexpected reply. 'He won't be far off, I should say. He *was* here, but somehow I seemed to upset him.'

Toad was most intrigued, but his discretion kept him moving. He would have dearly loved to have known what had happened at the meeting. Adder had never been known to consort with females, though his private activities were largely a mystery. But Toad was well aware that, even if he found his friend, the snake would give absolutely nothing away. He plodded on in a reflective mood.

From his solitary resting-place Adder heard the toad's rustlings through the leaves. He waited until he was closer and then made himself visible.

'You needn't have come looking for me,' he hissed.

'I didn't,' said Toad, 'I've had to abandon my little roost temporarily. I expect you can guess why.'

Adder's face was a mask. His impassive features did not show a flicker of comprehension. He remained silent. Toad said no more, but started to dig himself down into the leaf litter. His back feet worked vigorously.

'Are you burying yourself?' Adder asked curiously.

'Oh no. But I never squat quite on the surface,' Toad explained. 'You don't know what creature might come along.' He shot a sly glance at the snake but Adder made no response.

Later, when it was still dark but in the early part of the morning, they were aroused by the sound of running feet. They soon discovered the cause. It was Friendly and his group of followers.

'They look as if they have some purpose in mind,' Toad commented.

'Yesss,' drawled Adder. 'And I don't think it's a hunting trip.'

They watched the band of foxes move on their way.

'They don't often travel together like that,' Toad said. 'They've been on some errand or other.'

They had seen five of the foxes. Ranger had broken away to search for much-needed food. Some time afterwards he came right past the two animals, quite oblivious of their nearness. He was not one of the Farthing Wood community of creatures, but Toad and Adder were both impatient for information. So they halted him.

'Oh,' said Ranger, when he saw them. 'I hadn't realized. My mind was on other things.'

'We've just seen Friendly with a group of youngsters,' said Toad. 'Quite a bunch of them. We've been pondering the meaning of it.'

Ranger had no qualms about waiving secrecy, particularly as he had lost a lot of enthusiasm on this night for the idea of cornering the stranger. 'Yes, we made a party,' he told them honestly. 'We've been tracking the Beast.'

'I suppose you had no luck then,' Adder lisped, 'since there is no sign of any injuries?'

'We did and we didn't,' Ranger returned cryptically. 'It's all Friendly's idea. He wants to get the Beast away from here and he thinks a group of us can do it. I doubt if he's right. It escaped us easily. But I agree with him that *something* has to be done.'

Adder displayed his wounds in an elaborate exhibition of what could happen to them too. But they were lost for the most part on Ranger who, even in the moonlight, could scarcely see their severity.

'Do you mean to go on with this?' Toad asked the fox.

'Friendly wants to. I'm beginning to have doubts,' Ranger replied. 'But I'll stay with him a while and see what turns up.'

'I've just shown you what will turn up,' Adder hissed acidly. 'You won't be warned. So try and think of your offspring.'

'Oh, I have done,' Ranger assured him. 'But I have no control, you must understand. They're not cubs – any of them.'

'You're all cubs in temperament,' Adder told him bluntly. 'Playing around with something that could be lethal.'

Ranger objected to Adder's tone of superiority. He – Ranger – was no refugee from Farthing Wood who was obliged to respect the foibles of his comrades. 'You're entitled to your opinion,' he told the snake, 'for what it's worth. But I think the subject of tracking and out-manoeuvring a mammal is best left to those who know about these things.'

Adder was not in the least put out. He had the patience to wait for his words to be proved true by future events.

Ranger did not tarry. He wanted to get back to Charmer and see that all was safe with their new litter.

Charmer greeted him with her customary sweetness. She soon allayed his fears and then asked him if he and the others had been successful.

'No,' said Ranger. 'Not successful. Only the Beast continues to be that. He is a proficient hunter and I think will always evade any of our stumbling efforts.'

'The deer herd is very much in peril then,' Charmer surmised. 'How glad I am fox meat is no delicacy.' She shuddered as she looked at her cubs.

Ranger looked too, and the sight of the tiny bundles of fur huddling together for warmth steeled his resolve. Yes, Friendly was right. They *must* go on. For what sort of future could there be for these little ones – or any of them – whilst they were all in this stranger's power?

'The white stags must long for their new antlers to grow,' he murmured. 'They are the herd's only protection.' He lay down next to his mate. Charmer nuzzled him comfortingly. Outside the den, dawn hovered on the horizon.

At first light Adder stirred. Toad was deep in his bower of soft soil and leaves. The snake slid noiselessly away. The she-viper was again in his thoughts. Adder found himself moving in her direction. He had not decided what sort of approach he would use with her and, as he went along, he endeavoured to compose a really choice remark. But the female had gone on her way, and Adder was left to wonder about her – and ponder, his hurts forgotten.

*****

Later that day the Park's inhabitants became aware that some new scheme was being put into action by the Warden. He and three other men were working by the perimeter of the Reserve, on a piece of open ground about half a kilometre from the Warden's cottage. They did not at first realize what was happening, for the sight of men and their tools and machinery frightened them and they kept well away. But as the day went on, birds who flew over the area were able to report on events. It seemed that part of the Park was being cordoned off. Using the boundary fence on one side, an enclosure was being erected with extra poles and bars which looked like a miniature reserve within the Reserve. The curiosity of the animals was profound but, naturally, they dared not go anywhere near the work. By late afternoon it was complete. Whistler decided to go and have a look for the benefit of his own particular animal friends.

When the heron flew over the construction, the men had left taking all their equipment with them. Already a few of the most inquisitive beasts were gathering to make an inspection. From the air the fencing could be seen as forming a circle. There was a single opening.

'Now what on earth is it for?' Whistler asked himself. He made sure he looked at it from all sides, so that he could describe it accurately to the others. 'Something is to be put in it, that's clear.' He flew away, racking his brains for a solution.

Fox and Vixen, Weasel and Leveret were waiting for Whistler's return. When he told them, in the greatest detail, what he had seen, they put their heads together.

'It sounds like a sort of cage,' Vixen said.

'Of course!' cried Weasel. 'It must be for the Beast!'

'I don't think that can be, Weasel,' Whistler remarked. 'It's too big for one animal. And, besides, can't the creature climb?'

'Yes, yes. It wouldn't hold it,' Fox agreed. 'Something much more subtle would be needed for that cunning character.'

'It's not – er – something that all of us could be put into, is it?' Leveret asked hesitantly, afraid he would sound a fool.

The others were amused at the idea but tried not to show it.

'There would be no point in that,' Fox reassured the hare. 'Don't worry Leveret.'

A familiar hoot sounded and they looked up to see Tawny Owl flying towards them. He seemed to be in a great haste about something. He landed awkwardly, bumping into the heron's long legs and making the tall bird rock.

'Sorry, Whistler,' he muttered in a flustered way. 'The deer – the deer — ' he started to say. Then he stopped. 'I must remember my age – shouldn't fly so fast,' he murmured to himself.

'What of the deer?' Fox asked eagerly. It was obvious something of import had occurred.

'They're being – rounded up,' Owl told them with an effort. He had tired himself badly.

'So that's it!' the others cried simultaneously.

'Yes, there are men on horseback and – and – a couple of dogs,' Tawny Owl went on. 'I don't know where they mean to take them.'

Fox enlightened the bird. Then he continued, 'The men must want the whole herd in one place. Easier to look after them, I suppose.'

'They'll have to feed them as well,' Vixen pointed out, 'if they're not left free to forage.'

'Well, one thing's for certain,' said Weasel. 'It will call a halt to our silent friend's activities.' He spoke with great satisfaction.

'Yes, indeed,' said Whistler. 'But wait – this Beast could *still* get at them.'

'I think we should give the humans credit for a little more sense,' Fox said wryly. 'They're not likely to leave a herd of penned-up deer unguarded, are they? They're to be protected from its ravages, not left at its mercy.'

'Of course,' said the heron. 'How silly of me.'

'*And*,' Fox emphasized, 'there's another aspect. The deer might also act as bait to lead the Beast on. Then our clever Warden and his friends will pounce and – the threat is gone!'

'Poor deer,' murmured Vixen, 'to be used in such a way. I hope the Beast will show its cleverness again by seeing sense and leaving this hunting ground.'

As soon as Vixen had finished speaking she and all the others realized at once the implications of what she had said. They looked at one another with serious faces. The thought had occurred simultaneously to them. The Beast might decide not to leave, but simply to change its diet!

Leveret knew that he was the most vulnerable of the group then present. 'The likes of me and the rabbits will be its fare again,' he said in a whisper, looking ahead with frightened eyes as if he could visualize this nightmare. 'None of you are at such risk from it – nor have you ever been.'

'We must try and look on the bright side,' Fox told him earnestly. 'If the Beast has developed a taste for deer, then it might not wish to forgo the treat. So, what happens? It is captured – or destroyed.'

'I'm not convinced,' Leveret replied. 'Thank you for your encouragement, Fox. I know you mean well. But, you see, there's something about this creature – a kind of – er – invincibility.'

'Well, we'll see about that,' Fox said grimly. 'In the

meantime, you and your family must lie low and not stray too far.'

'Oh, we've been doing that all along,' Leveret said. 'But *that's* no defence.'

'Leveret's right,' said Tawny Owl. He turned to the hare. 'I don't know why you can't take a lesson from your rabbit cousins and get yourself underground. You lie out in the open with no more than a depression in the ground to hide you.' He never was the most tactful of beings and Weasel gave him a glare that told him just that.

'We're not diggers, Owl,' Leveret explained simply. 'We have to rely on our speed.'

Tawny Owl stared back at Weasel, quite unrepentant. Then he went on in the same vein. He made a virtue of bluntness. 'You'd need some speed, too,' he commented, turning once more to the hare, 'to get away from the creature *I* saw.'

Weasel was exasperated. 'What do you know about it?' he demanded. 'Was the Beast running when you saw it?'

'Er – no, but I – '

'Well, don't talk such nonsense then,' Weasel interrupted him. 'Leveret's a timid enough animal as it is.'

Tawny Owl did seem to feel a twinge of regret. 'I just think it's better to know the facts,' he excused himself. 'I'm sure Leveret understands. I wasn't trying to frighten him.'

'It's all right,' said the hare. 'Don't let's argue – that won't help. We're all in this together, aren't we?'

'Of course we are,' said Tawny Owl promptly. 'If I can be of any assistance at all you know you can always count on me.'

'Except for any diplomacy,' Weasel muttered.

'Tell me, Owl,' Whistler said hastily, 'are you still of the mind that there is more than one strange beast about?'

Tawny Owl had forgotten his own theory on that matter. 'Oh – er – well, I can't be certain about it, Whistler. The facts are beginning to point, I suppose, to there being – er – perhaps just the one.'

He had been caught off guard and felt a trifle awkward about it. He tried to retrieve the situation. 'Anyway,' he said, 'I'll keep an eye open tonight by this – um – deer pen and see if I can discover anything.' The animals watched him fly away.

'Well,' said Fox. 'The next few days should tell us if the Warden's plan will work out or not. The craft of the Beast will really be put to the test.'

—9—
Captured

Before dusk, Friendly was ready and waiting for the evening's action. The three younger foxes – Pace, Rusty and Husky – arrived just as darkness began to steal across the Park. Ranger and Trip came last. No word was spoken. They all knew what they were going to do.

Husky took the lead, with Pace and Rusty behind him. They made straight for the fawn's remains they had found the night before. As they neared the place they slowed and went much more carefully. As usual, they paused periodically to listen. They reached the carcass. There were only bones and skin left. Friendly sniffed vigorously at the carcass and then at the ground all about. The others followed suit.

'The smell of blood is very strong,' Friendly said in a low voice. 'And there's something else – something recognizable.' He was thoroughly absorbed. 'Yes, it's the same as before. It's the creature's scent all right. The question is – where does it lead?' With his muzzle bent low, he moved about, this way and that, making patterns over the ground. Then he gave a bark of excitement. 'Come on,' he whispered. 'This way!'

He was following the strongest scent; the one made most recently. The other foxes followed him through the undergrowth. The youngsters' hearts were beating wildly.

'Keep your eyes and ears at full alert,' Friendly turned to say. 'Leave the tracking to me.'

They went on slowly. The undergrowth gave way to open grassy ground. Much of it was still soft from the frequent spring showers of rain. Suddenly, Friendly stopped. He turned round. His eyes were glistening. 'Look!' he said triumphantly.

Amongst the short grass there was a small patch of bare earth dotted with plantain. In the centre of it, almost as if left deliberately to assist them, was a huge pawprint.

'We're really on to something, this time,' said Friendly. 'Here's an unmistakable clue.'

They all stared at it. It seemed obvious that it had been made quite recently. Only Ranger seemed unhappy. 'I don't know,' he said. 'It could be a trap.'

'A trap!' cried the young foxes together.

'What are you getting at, Ranger?' Friendly asked him quietly.

'Isn't it too obvious a clue?' he returned.

'Nonsense!' was Friendly's immediate reaction. 'Do you mean it's trying to lure us –' He broke off. He looked at Ranger and considered. 'There may be something in that,' he murmured. 'How are we to tell?' He was pensive for a while. Then he shook himself out of his reverie. 'Anyway, if you're correct,' he said, 'then so be it.' Friendly looked determined. 'Our friend will find he has more than he bargained for.'

The foxes proceeded on the trail but with noticeably more caution. They crossed the open ground and now the scent led them under some trees. They found themselves in a small copse. It was not one they had been to before. Pace, Rusty and Husky were feeling the strain of having their eyes and ears as it were stretched to their limit. Ranger and Trip showed no sign of their feelings, but they all were expecting something to happen. Friendly came to a stop at the foot of a tree. He went round the tree, trying to trace where the scent led. Then he sat down, looking puzzled. The rest of the group regarded him, but could not find their voices. The skin on their backs began to crawl. Slowly they raised their heads.

Friendly followed their eyes and, as he did so, a most unearthly snarl ripped through the stillness of the copse. In the next instant a huge creature leapt from the tree and landed directly beside Husky. With a vicious blow from a front paw it tumbled the fox over. The beast's jaws fastened on the scruff of his neck and he was lifted helplessly, legs dangling, as with one bound the creature whirled around and vaulted back into the tree. Its claws raked the bark as it raced up the trunk to its vantage point in a broad lofty branch. The five foxes barked furiously from the ground. Their fur was raised, their lips curled back to reveal their fangs, while their eyes gleamed with anger. But they were helpless. The beast retained its grip on the struggling Husky as securely as if he had been no more than a rabbit. There was a look of malevolence about the creature as it glared down at them which made their barks sputter into silence. The foxes were helpless and they knew it.

'It was – a trap,' Ranger muttered almost inaudibly. They stared up through the darkness, aware of their utter powerlessness in the face of this monster. All they could see was its shining eyes – eyes that seemed to mock their weakness. For some time they remained rooted to the spot. They were unable to think of any action they could take. They felt as if the Beast's influence had frozen their limbs into immobility.

At last Friendly said hoarsely, 'We must get help.' He had no idea what help they could look for, nor where they could look for it. It was a blind reaction from their situation put into words.

'But we can't leave . . . .' began Pace. His voice faltered and he lapsed into silence.

None of the others spoke. They dared not look at each other. Then, with drooping head, Friendly began to move away. He knew that, even if they should stay there until dawn, they could achieve nothing. The others followed him forlornly. From his terrifying height Husky witnessed their departure with the keenest agony.

As soon as the Beast was satisfied that the foxes had gone on their way, it released its grip. Husky fell like a stone to the ground.

When they were some distance from the copse the foxes began to give vent to their feelings. The natural course was to look for a culprit to blame for what had happened. So it followed that Friendly became the target.

'It was very foolhardy to come on this venture,' said Trip. 'It was your idea, Friendly. You might have known it could only end like this.'

'I guessed it would be a mistake from the start,' Ranger

concurred. 'Now see what you've led us into.'

'How shall we tell Whisper?' murmured Rusty.

Only Pace, Friendly's own son, forbore to comment. Yet his thoughts matched the others'.

'Don't you think I regret it now?' Friendly said miserably. 'But how could I have foreseen what has occurred? I did this from the best of motives. And – you didn't have to accompany me; none of you.'

'It's true,' said Pace. 'We must be fair. And it's too late to regret our actions.'

'We have to think of finding help,' Friendly said. '*I* don't know where to turn. Perhaps my father – '

'Your father,' Ranger cut in, 'would have had more sense at the outset!' (Now he recalled Adder's words.)

'You're right,' Friendly said unhappily. 'He gave his advice, at the beginning. "Don't meddle," he said.'

'Grandfather is very wise,' said Pace. 'He may think of something that can be done.'

They carried on their way in silence. In their minds was the picture of Husky clenched in the fierce jaws of the Beast – the powerful beast they had tried to tamper with! For Friendly the image held the most horror, for he did feel responsible despite what he had said.

Ranger and Trip left the group as they came near the earth of the Farthing Wood Fox. They were of a different parentage and had not the same allegiance.

Fox and Vixen were absent. Friendly gave a yelp of frustration. Just when he needed them most! Of course, they were hunting. However his call of distress brought another animal's answer. Friendly knew it was Badger's cry. He dearly loved the old creature but – ironically – he was the one friend who was really too old and feeble now to be of any assistance.

'What is it, Friendly?' Badger asked after greeting him and the two youngsters.

The fox explained with a woeful expression. Badger was aghast.

'Oh dear, oh dear, oh my word!' he muttered continually. He swung his striped head to and fro. 'Oh, Friendly!' he said. 'Oh dear, oh dear!' He was trying to think how he could help. 'Poor Husky. Has he a mate?'

'No,' Rusty answered.

'Well, that's a blessing,' Badger murmured. 'But Whisper will be so upset! Vixens are all the same when their cubs are in danger.' A though struck him. 'She mustn't be told – not yet,' he said hurriedly. 'She might do something foolish, and we've had enough foolishness already.'

Friendly took the implied reproof without demur.

Badger was beginning to think of an idea. It depended on what the Cat would do with its victim. If it intended killing Husky, then it was already too late for any animal to act. But if it merely meant to keep him captive, there perhaps was a way out. Badger made up his mind. He knew he could not tell the foxes his plan. They would be sure to prevent it. So he gave no sign.

'I think you must wait and speak to your father,' he told Friendly. 'No doubt you intended to do that anyway. You must all stay here. I'll see if I can find him and then I'll send him back to you. Now, you mustn't stray – do you promise?'

'We promise,' said Pace and Rusty. Friendly was too dispirited even to answer.

Badger shambled away, his head full of what he must do. It was some time before the realization struck him that he did not know where he was going. He did not know where Husky was!

'Oh, you old fool,' he castigated himself. 'You forgot to

find out where it all happened.' Now what could he do? He could not traverse the entire Park in search of the elusive hunter. And he could not go back to Friendly with the all-important question. He would be suspicious at once and then his plan would come to nothing. He had not meant really to look for Fox. He only wanted Fox's three relatives to remain where they were, out of the way. He knew that Fox and Vixen would return eventually of their own accord. But now he could think of nothing better to do than to consult his old friend himself. So he shuffled about, going to all the places he thought most likely to find him, and calling at intervals in his gruff, wheezy voice. He even went up to the stream and along the bank for a stretch in case Fox was after a meal of water-rat. But he saw nobody, not even Whistler, who was comfortably at roost in a tall tree at that time.

Badger, thoroughly disheartened, made his slow way back again. He hoped to find all the foxes together now. He was so wrapped up in his thoughts on the matter that he did not see a small creature move quickly out of his path. But he heard it squeak.

'Mole?' he mumbled automatically.

'No. Er – yes. Here I am, Badger,' was the answer. It was Mossy.

'Oh Mole, what trouble,' Badger said. 'Things have taken a turn for the worse. Husky has been captured by that awful Cat.'

Mossy did not know who Husky was, but he remembered Weasel's advice and made a pretence. 'Poor creature,' he commented, wondering for what sort of creature he was showing sympathy.

'Yes,' said Badger. 'They shouldn't have gone near it. And he's only a youngster.'

'I know,' fibbed Mossy.

'If this had to happen to one of us, why couldn't it have been me – or – or – somebody like me,' said Badger. 'My life's as good as over anyway.'

'Don't say that, Badger,' shrilled Mossy, more genuinely. 'Your friends would be heartbroken.'

'Well, thank you, dear Mole,' Badger said warmly. 'But – oh! I must leave you now. There's no time to waste.'

Mossy watched Badger lumber away and he felt a surge of affection for the old animal. 'He was the truest of friends to my father, I know,' he murmured to himself. 'Perhaps I can help repay the debt.'

As soon as he was within sight of Fox and Vixen's earth once more, Badger noticed that they had come back. All five foxes were in conclave – Friendly, Pace and Rusty anxiously explaining what had happened. Badger paused awhile in order that the bad news would have been grasped, with all its implications, before he joined them. When he did do so, Vixen turned a miserably worried face in his direction. Fox was deep in his own thoughts. Only when Badger was amongst them did he see Tawny Owl looking on from a nearby perch. He wondered if Owl had had something to report too. Now he felt he must ask his question.

'Where is Husky? Where did it take place?'

In a low voice Pace described the copse. Badger pumped him for more information. What quarter of the Park? Was it near the boundary fence?

'Nowhere near that,' Tawny Owl chimed in. 'The Warden is in that area, guarding the deer. So the Beast is keeping well away. In any case, it would have no need to risk being shot.'

'No. There's other food,' Badger agreed. Then he wished he had not. He had been thinking of rabbits and such like, but now he wondered about Husky.

'Not only other food,' Owl continued, 'but its preferred food.'

Badger was puzzled. 'Preferred food?' he repeated.

'Oh yes. Not all the deer have been penned, you know. I've seen two hinds wandering free, quite on their own. They must have wandered off and become separated. Probably old ones past breeding.'

Now Fox looked up. 'You see, human ingenuity has failed too, Badger. What hope have *we* of ridding ourselves of this pest?'

'Well, we can't live life as if we're under siege,' Badger declared. 'And first of all we must rescue Husky.'

'Do tell us how you propose to do so,' Tawny Owl begged. He was convinced Badger was becoming senile and he waited to hear a stream of nonsense.

'I do have a plan,' said Badger uncertainly. 'But I – I – can't tell you it.'

Tawny Owl made derisive noises. But Fox was interested.

'Why can't you tell us?' he queried.

'You wouldn't approve,' Badger explained.

'He's got some madcap notion of challenging the Beast to combat, I suppose,' Owl remarked scornfully.

Badger remained silent. There was a grain of truth in what he had said but he had not quite hit the mark.

'I hope that's not – ' Fox began urgently.

'No, no, don't worry,' Badger assured him. 'I'm not quite the old idiot Owl takes me for.'

'I didn't say that,' Owl remarked, a little embarrassed.

Badger now pretended to have taken great offence. It suited his plan. 'And you're so sharp, aren't you, Owl?' he growled. 'You couldn't even recognize the creature as being a big Cat!' He made a great play of looking very hurt and indignant and turned his back on them all.

'Now look what you've done,' Fox said angrily to Tawny Owl. 'Do you have to make even more trouble? As if we haven't enough to contend with!'

'Well – I – I – never intended . . . .' the bird spluttered.

When Badger was sure he was hidden by the darkness, he put on speed. He knew he had to act quickly, because he was sure Fox would eventually demand that Friendly lead him and Vixen to the scene of Husky's capture. He could not simply do nothing. It was not in Fox's nature. So, armed with only the scant descriptions Pace had given him, Badger trundled forward in search of the copse. His idea was a simple one – to offer himself in exchange for the release of Husky.

—10—
A Common Aim

Fox had, indeed, accepted that there was no alternative but to go to help, and at length the four male foxes went on their way. Vixen left Tawny Owl for Badger's set. She wanted to console him for the hurt she supposed he had taken. The set, of course, was empty. As Vixen emerged from Badger's dark labyrinth she found Mossy apparently on his way there.

'Is Badger there?' he asked. He knew who Vixen was.

'No, Oh – you must be – '

'I'm to be known simply as "Mole",' he twittered informatively.

'Of course.'

Mossy began to ask Vixen about Husky. He soon discovered he was another fox. Then he told her what Badger had said about his life being almost over, and how it would have been better if *he* had been the captured animal. Vixen went cold. She recalled Badger asking Pace for directions. Yes, there was no doubt of his intentions – it would be typical of him. She must stop him!

She raced away. Her first idea was to use Tawny Owl as her messenger. Wings were faster than legs. But Owl was nowhere to be seen now and she had to trust to her own speed. Vixen was no longer the swift-footed, lithe creature of her youth. She loped along for a while, then eased down to a trot. If she could catch up with the other four, one of the young foxes could be sent on to forestall Badger. But her breathing became laboured and soon she had to stop altogether, her sides heaving, to bring it under control.

Badger's lead had been cut considerably by Friendly's faster pace. But the old animal lumbered on persistently, full of dogged determination. He was not absolutely sure of his destination and, because of this, the foxes on their direct course arrived at the scene first. Friendly led them, with much trepidation, towards the tree where the killer had lurked. Husky's body lay where it had fallen, all life crushed out of it. Friendly stared at it in horror and disbelief. The others surrounded him.

Fox looked at his dead grandson. He remembered, with a sharp pang, another occasion when he had found one of his own cubs in just such a state. The only difference this time was that the body was full grown. And there were no marks on it.

Pace and Rusty were looking fearfully up into the tree. No sound, no sign hinted at the presence of the hunter.

The Cat had done its work and had moved on – who knew where?

Vixen was next to arrive. Fox looked at his mate without speaking.

'Are – are we too late?' Vixen whispered. Then she saw the still form of Husky.

'He never had a chance,' Fox rasped. He was racked by helpless, impotent anger. 'I will get even,' he intoned in a growl to himself.

Vixen understood. She could find nothing to say. Her heart ached.

'It was a desire to get even that began it all,' Friendly muttered. 'I didn't think – oh how ignorant I was!'

'Let's get away from here,' Rusty suggested. The sight of Husky's body frightened him. He knew how easily it could have been himself lying there.

'Yes – it's a hateful place,' said Fox.

'We must wait for Badger,' Vixen said hurriedly as they began to move.

They looked at her questioningly. 'He – he thought he could help,' she explained lamely. There was no need now to go into detail.

'So that was why he wanted the directions,' Pace remarked. 'Dear old Badger – this is no quarrel of his.'

'Of course it is,' Fox told him surprisingly. 'Any quarrel of mine has always been Badger's too. He'll soon tell you that.'

Badger came at last, grunting, and out of breath. He saw, in his turn, the young animal he had set out to save. 'It really has gone too far now, hasn't it?' he muttered.

'But what are we to do, Badger?' Friendly wailed.

'Wage a war,' was the old animal's reply. His voice suddenly seemed to have lost its wheeziness. It sounded crisp, assertive and younger.

'*I* tried,' said the fox. 'Look what I've achieved.'

'You should not have acted alone,' Badger admonished him. 'There are those who are wiser and more experienced than yourself. They should have been consulted.' He named no names.

The Farthing Wood Fox spoke. He was unaccustomed to finding himself put in the shade by Badger and he admired his resolution. 'Well, old friend,' he said, 'this isn't the first time we've faced danger. Where do we begin?'

Vixen did not like the tone the talk was taking. She saw the cause as hopeless. 'How can you begin anywhere?' she cried. 'How can you fight an enemy you can't see and know nothing about? None of us, separately or together, is a match for this beast.'

'Are we to wait about then, all of us, to be picked off one by one?' Fox demanded. 'Is that what you want?'

'No, no,' said Vixen. 'But I don't want any more deaths either.'

'Deaths are inevitable,' Fox declared. 'There will continue to be killings until this threat is eradicated.'

'Oh, you've changed,' she told him. 'You said yourself, before, we shouldn't meddle . . . .'

'Yes, I've changed,' Fox admitted coldly. 'That pathetic sight at the foot of the tree changed me.'

Vixen knew her mate. His mind was made up. Now, she feared, there would be no end to their troubles. She clung to one faint hope. Human intelligence. Somehow the Warden would find the Big Cat before they did.

The animals left the copse. Fox was already formulating ideas for a campaign. He would need all the help and support he could muster. – not just from the old community of Farthing Wood, but all their dependants;

all the birds he could find willing to scour the Reserve by day and night; the other larger mammals of the Park – every creature who could play a part. Before anything else they *had* to locate the Cat and note its movements; otherwise there might be a massacre. How he wished he could count on the strength of the white deer herd. The stags, with their antlers grown, would be formidable contestants. But they were out of the reckoning now, bottled up in one corner in a fruitless attempt by Man to frustrate the Beast's activities.

They reached their home territory. 'Put the word about,' he told the other foxes. 'All the animals in the park must be united in this. I want to have any slightest clue reported. Whistler and Owl must speak to the birds. We ourselves must assemble in the Hollow tomorrow at dusk – every one of us. That includes the vixens. Every animal will be needed. We *must* involve everyone from the largest to the smallest. We all know the risks. But risks are preferable to subjection. And that's what we're experiencing.'

Fox was his old self. Like Badger, he seemed suddenly to have thrown off the seasons. He was a leader again. The younger foxes marvelled and ran off unquestioningly to do his bidding. Fox waited for Tawny Owl to put in an appearance and, when he did, told him what he wanted. Owl recognized the urgency in his voice and the note of command. He respected Fox above all others and bowed to his authority. He noticed Badger watching and regretted that they were at loggerheads.

'Oh – um – Badger,' he hooted, 'you know, I never meant to – um – give the impression – er – well, that you – '

'It's all right, Owl,' Badger called up to him. 'Think nothing of it. We're all apt to say things at times.'

'Thank you, Badger,' said Tawny Owl in an unusually humble manner. 'Are we still friends?'

'Oh, Owl,' said Badger. 'Have we ever been anything else?'

Tawny Owl gave a hoot of pleasure and flew away.

At dusk on the following day the Farthing Wood animals gathered with their kindred. Whisper, Husky's mother, had been told of his death and was near the front of the gathering. The other vixens, among them Charmer and Russet, Friendly's mate, were there too. Fox explained how the entire Reserve must be alerted. Together they could drive the stranger from their home. Whisper's loss was alleviated a little by the proposal for action. She wanted to have a leading role in avenging her cub.

Over the next few days and nights, the animals and birds of White Deer Park became aware that all of them were to be part of a concerted move to restore their habitat to safety. Despite day-to-day differences which arose from the natural order of things, they realized that on this issue they were as one. All of them knew of the existence of the stranger and feared it. They had needed something to be done and had only lacked a leader. Now in Fox they had been given one: a co-ordinator for their scheme. They were glad – and relieved – to be doing something positive. So all over the Reserve the animals and birds kept watch at all times for a sign of the Cat. They waited for it to make a move, some by day and some in the darkness.

Each night the Warden or another man patrolled near the deer pen, unwitting allies of the animal community. For a while there was nothing to report. There were no more killings. This lapse was unexpected. Had the Beast gone away of its own choice? Or was it using its cunning again to lull them into a false sense of security?

The deer still at loose in the Park were aware of their vulnerability and kept constantly on the move, never staying in one area for long, and ranging through the whole of the Reserve. One of them was found near the pen one night and persuaded, with the use of a stick, to join its fellows. Then the gate was securely fastened again behind it.

The deer herd did not relish their confinement. They had no escape route if their attacker should decide to put in an appearance by day. They suspected that the Cat could vault the enclosure and create havoc amongst them if it should choose. They felt unsafe and had no faith in the humans' ability to protect them. They would have preferred to take their chance and roam free when they at least had the use of their legs to run from danger. However, it was soon proved that *they* were not to be the target, but the one deer still at large.

Somehow the Cat had eluded every effort to locate it. Of course there was nothing to stop it going in and out of the Park at will, and none of the animals was quite sure just what its movements were. It never allowed even a hint to come their way. Then at last the solitary hind was stalked and pulled down as she drank by the stream in the evening. The Beast was hungry and ate a hearty meal, leaving part of the deer well hidden amongst a mass of waterside vegetation for its return later. The kill was not witnessed, but the carcass was discovered by a moorhen paddling about amongst the reeds. Whistler was soon made aware of it and gradually the Park heard that the Beast was back in action. They tried again – keeping eyes peeled, ears open for a clue.

Meanwhile the Warden had come to the realization that the ruse of penning the deer was not going to work. The hunter was too clever to come near and there was no benefit to the deer themselves, who were becoming fretful and difficult to feed. So the barricades came down and the nightly vigils were ended. The deer ran free again and exulted in the feeling. The Warden was reduced to tramping over the Reserve again in daylight hours. He was becoming convinced that the threat was over. Fox and his associates knew better.

'It's beaten us again,' he complained to Vixen. 'How does it manage it?'

'It's a superior creature,' she answered. 'Superior in cunning, superior in hunting, superior in every way. Husky's name for the Beast was "Stealth", and stealth is the essence of the animal. It has a sort of stealth that we cannot begin to understand.'

'And with all of us – every animal around – out looking for it! The humans are beaten too. Where *does* it go?'

With the deer herd available again as an unlimited food source, the Cat had no need to return to the place of its last kill. So the motley collection of birds and animals who had that corner under special scrutiny had no reward for their pains. However, at last a sort of clue did emerge from an unexpected source.

Adder had not encountered the surprising she-viper again. After their first meeting he had not felt that he had given a very good account of himself and he wished he could put that right. He felt she had somehow got the better of him and he could not feel comfortable about it. As time went on he did not think a lot about her but when he did she still intrigued him.

The weather was now quite warm. All the trees were in leaf; there was new greenery everywhere. Adder had his favourite spots for basking and one of these was a piece of sloping ground, not a great distance from the stream. It was well screened by fronds of bracken. The bed of last year's brown dead fern fronds underneath him made the ground warm and, among the new fast-growing green

shoots, Adder delighted to indulge himself, particularly
after eating. He had thought this place was his and his
entirely. But one day, after swallowing a vole and feeling
very sleepy, he had slid into the spot, only to find another
occupant. This did not please him and he said grumpily,
'How long have you been coming here?' He was talking
to the she-viper.

She stared at him in the snake's usual unblinking way.
But her tongue tested Adder for smell. 'Oh – the scarred
one,' was her response. 'But no,' she added. 'Am I
mistaken? Or have the wounds healed?'

'Of course they've healed; they were only scratches,'
Adder hissed. 'And you haven't answered my question.'

'Coming here? Not very long. I found this spot by
chance.'

'Did you though? Well, I might tell you that I've been
sunning myself here without interference from another
for as long as – '

'I'm not going to interfere with your habits,' she
interrupted. 'There's plenty of room for both of us.'

'I like solitude,' Adder asserted. (As soon as he had said
it he wondered why he had.) 'And I have a prior
claim.'

'You make yourself understood,' the female replied
drily. 'I take the hint. There's plenty of room in the Park.'
She uncoiled herself and began to slide away. Before she
disappeared she said, 'You may like to know, Solitude-
lover, that this isn't necessarily the safest of places for
you.'

Adder checked her departure. 'How do you mean?' he
lisped.

'I mean that, in view of your previous tussle, you
possibly wouldn't want to risk another one.'

'Are you referring to the Cat?'

'Indeed I am,' she answered. 'I know for a fact that it

sometimes uses a large hole in the bank by the water's edge for concealment. The hole is well covered and not many know about it. Who can say if the creature is there now?'

'How do you know all this?' Adder asked, thinking of the way all the inhabitants of the park had been baffled by the stranger's secrecy.

'Quite by accident,' the female snake informed him. 'It can only be seen from the stream and I happened to be following a frog.'

'But why haven't you told anyone?' Adder demanded. 'I assume you've been involved in the general alert?'

'But I have told someone now, haven't I?' she answered disarmingly. 'Because I thought you needed to know.'

Her final remark had scarcely registered its message before she was gone. Adder was left to brood in his solitude, unsure whether he was glad or sorry she had left. He felt strangely restless. He had never experienced uncertainty about himself before.

—11—
United

Adder did no sunbathing that day. He pulled himself together and set off for the stream, but with the she-viper's caution very much in his mind. He wanted to investigate the lair in the bank. Once in the water, Adder felt he was safe. He swam in one direction, close to the edge of the stream, looking for places where the vegetation was thickest. He saw no hole large enough for the Cat to get into so, despite his feeling of chill, he swam across to the other bank and reversed his direction. He was becoming colder and colder and his movements slower and slower. He knew he would soon have to abandon the stream and search for warmth. Then he saw it – a dark opening in the bank almost obscured by reeds and rushes. He could see at once that its cavernous depths would easily accommodate a whole group of animals. Adder swam on by. He was not such a fool as to approach any closer. The darkness of the hole would comfortably hide whatever creature might be inside it.

When he was far enough away from the lair, the snake slid from the stream and up the bank. He was quite torpid from the cold, and allowed himself to revive in the sun's warmth, only a metre or so from the water. When he was ready, he rippled away at his swiftest pace to carry the news of his sighting. He was hoping to find Whistler the heron before anyone else. The bird could act as his messenger.

He found him without difficulty, and quickly explained about the hole in the bank and of its importance. He said nothing of the she-viper, but only that 'another animal' had given him the clue. It seemed that Whistler had no idea that the hole was there.

'I look downwards at the water, you see,' he told Adder, 'so I'd be looking the wrong way.'

'Yes,' said the snake. 'The hole faces the stream so, unless you could swim, you wouldn't discover it.'

'Well,' said Whistler, 'at last we've got something to get to work on. I'll tell Fox.'

Adder composed himself to wait, while the tall bird spread his wings. Fox received the information with grim satisfaction.

'Good,' he said. 'Now we'll gather as many together as we can and we'll have the resources to beard our friend in his own den.'

Once again Vixen was wary. 'I wish we could leave this to the humans,' she said. 'The Cat is sure to kill another deer sooner or later, and then they'll be combing the Park for it.'

'We can't trust to that,' Fox answered. 'It would almost certainly elude them again. Anyway, we know what they don't know. We've found its hidey-hole.'

'From what Adder told me, this lair seems to be used only periodically,' Whistler said.

'That's enough,' said Fox easily. 'We're bound to catch him at home some time.' Then he turned to Vixen again and said softly to her, with all his old affection, 'You've been a wonderful mate to me – no fox could have asked for a better one. I've always listened to your advice. But we've always looked after our own and our age doesn't alter our obligations. Husky's death makes it necessary for us to take some action now, when before we might have stood aloof. I have been thinking of Bold. Remember how he wore out his own life to ensure that Husky and his other offspring should be born here – in what he believed was a haven. I feel we owe his memory something.'

Vixen's eyes melted as she looked at him and, for a brief moment, she and Fox were lost in their own private world. Whistler stepped awkwardly away on his long thin legs. Neither of the foxes spoke any more but Vixen had given her answer.

It took some time for the animals to gather, for word of the discovery had to be taken around from creature to creature. By the evening, however, there was a large assemblage outside Fox's earth, while new arrivals swelled the numbers all the time. There were creatures of all sizes – foxes, badgers, stoats, hares, rabbits, squirrels, hedgehogs, weasels, even mice and frogs. In the nearby trees there were owls, rooks, magpies, crows, thrushes, jays, blackbirds, starlings and tree sparrows. The Farthing Wood animals and their kin kept in a group together. All of them had come, including the smallest – Toad and Mossy. Whilst none of these assembled animals would have had the temerity to act of their own accord, they felt safe in the heart of the gathering, and even appeared to be enjoying themselves. Only the deer herd had stayed apart. The deer were convinced that they were the true quarry of the hunter, and therefore served their own purpose best by staying together and trying to protect each other.

During the night there were more arrivals. Fox was content to wait until dawn. He knew the Beast was active principally by night. So the most likely time to catch it unawares was by day when it would probably be resting. In the darkness many of the animals slept. At first light, Fox was ready to move. With Vixen alongside, and with all their relatives behind them, he set off for the stream. After the foxes came Badger, Weasel and Leveret. The rest of the creatures followed them, the largest at the forefront. Overhead the birds flapped, with Whistler at their head.

Adder's first realization that something was happening was the sight of the heron accompanied by Tawny Owl, with birds of all sizes strung out in their rear.

'It's begun,' was Whistler's announcement to the snake. 'You never saw such a collection.'

Adder made no comment. He was waiting for Fox. When he saw him approaching he slid forward. It was still early morning.

'You've chosen a good time,' the snake remarked. 'A short while ago I saw the Cat slaking its thirst downstream.'

'How far?' Fox asked at once.

'Oh, not far. About as far as the lair lies from here.'

'Then the game is on,' Fox murmured.

The animals moved on at their varying paces. The most timid of them experienced a feeling of security in the company of fiercer creatures that was quite unlike the normal pattern of their existence. For they all knew that there was but one aim in all their minds.

Adder guided the leaders as far as he dared. He indicated the mass of vegetation that clothed the entrance hole. It was indeed perfectly hidden from observation. Fox went down the bank and stepped gingerly into the water. Keeping near the shore he paddled out just far enough to see the lair for himself. Nothing could be detected inside. No sound issued from the den. He returned to the bank.

'Well, we must assume our friend is there,' he said. 'We have no proof.'

Many of the animals began to question him about his tactics. Would he go in? Would he wait for the Beast to come out? What were *they* to do in the meantime?

'There's nothing to do at present,' Fox told them. 'We have to be sure.' He looked thoughtful. What was needed was for one of the smallest creatures, and one who could swim well, to get as close as was necessary without being noticed. But how could he ask for a volunteer? As it turned out, he did not have to. Toad had come forward himself.

'I'll soon find out if he's in there,' he offered boldly.

'Are you sure, Toad?' Fox asked his friend dubiously. 'You see, it would mean going some way into the hole itself to be certain. I don't want to send you to – '

'Don't be concerned,' Toad interrupted. He had not bargained for doing any more than having a little swim, but he thought it would look cowardly now to withdraw. 'Is the Beast,' he continued, 'going to take any notice of a tiny inedible mouthful such as me?' He tried to sound humorous.

'Perhaps you're right,' Fox answered. 'But I'm still not very happy about it. Please, Toad, do use the utmost care!'

'Of course I will,' said Toad as he moved to the edge of the bank. Then, with a little kick from his hind legs, he jumped into the water. His small body hardly disturbed the surface. He swam in short spurts to the lair entrance and pulled himself out on to the muddy strand. Then, a few centimetres at a time, he crawled into the darkness.

Toad was probably the most suited of all the animals for the job. He was small and therefore light-footed, unexcitable, and naturally unhurried and quiet in his movements. Once he had left the stream he was hidden from view, and all the animals waited with bated breath in an unaccustomed stillness. Fox, above all, longed for Toad to reappear.

Time crept by. There was no sign of Toad. Fox began to fear the worst. Then, as if he had been engaged on nothing more serious than a pleasurable splash around, he was seen slowly swimming upstream, against the current, to where the others were assembled.

'Took rather longer – than I thought,' said Toad, arriving a bit short of breath. 'I had to – go in a long way. It's very dark; not much light gets in to see by. I could hear breathing – deep and steady, typical of a mammal when it's asleep. That gave me the confidence to go closer. The breathing got louder so I knew I was getting near. Then I saw a shape, curled up. I could make no more of it – too dark, you see. I wondered whether to leave then. But I thought – what's the good of that? I still don't know what's here.'

Toad paused for a rest..He was enjoying being the focus of attention and wanted to make the most of his story. Then he went on.

'I decided the only thing I could do was to go right up to the sleeper. So I did and I hopped all round, and it took me quite a while just to do that. I can tell you, the thing is enormous! It has silky fur, like a cat's – some of the hairs brushed me as I made my inspection. By then I was sure enough. No other creature of its size lives in *this* Park, except for the deer, and I know it wasn't one of them. So I left – slowly and cautiously. The breathing sounded the same. I heard nothing else. So I don't think I could have woken it. Now I don't know what you plan to do, Fox, but we should do something soon. The animal is there. We can seal off its exit and – we have it at bay!'

Toad's courageous deed was obscured by the urgency of taking action together. But it was not quite so simple, as Fox told him.

'We can't all stand or swim around in the water, Toad, waiting for it to come out. That's one escape route we can't deny it.'

'What about the strand?' Toad asked.

'How big is it?'

'Big enough for a few of the largest animals such as yourself to station yourselves there.'

'That's no use, then,' Fox commented. 'A few would just be tossed aside.'

'What shall we do then?'

'We must find out if there's another entrance to this lair. I think it unlikely the Cat would always get in from the water.'

Fox went off along the bank. He wanted to try and get in under the vegetation to see if there was an opening on the land side. The animals watched him go. They were keyed up, and some of the more highly-strung amongst them were no longer able to keep still. Rabbits and various groups of mice began to jump about nervously, wishing they had not come. It was quite apparent that the stranger would only have to show itself for them to turn tail and bolt.

Fox had set himself the most difficult of tasks. He did not want to rouse the sleeper. Yet it was quite impossible for him to avoid making a noise as he pushed himself into the clumps of growth. He thrust about with his muzzle, pausing tensely after each rustle and swish. Finally he managed to nose his way into the heart of the greenery. If there *was* another entrance he knew he might suddenly come face to face with the Beast, for every slight noise he made was magnified by his own fear. But he found nothing, though he made as thorough a search as he could.

As Fox was withdrawing from this screen he heard a noise break out; a noise of many voices. Animal and bird cries swelled in pitch and he knew something was astir. Above it all he could hear Vixen calling him and he hastily pulled himself clear. He imagined all sorts of horrors, but what he actually saw was so unexpected that it brought him to a halt. The collection of animals had pulled back, even the foxes. It seemed their confidence en masse had been a short-lived thing. Some of the rabbits had begun to run away, and were now paused at some distance, trying to gauge the situation. The smallest creatures – the mice and frogs – had already disappeared. And there, calmly seated by the waterside, was the Cat, watching them all with an expression of total disinterest. As Fox went by, the creature stretched each of its limbs luxuriously and then began to wash itself. It paid them less attention then if they had been a swarm of flies.

Fox joined Vixen at the head of the throng. He looked back at the stranger. It was a magnificent animal. Its body was clothed in glossy golden brown fur with darker blotches. It had long legs, a small compact head with rounded ears, and a long thick banded tail with a blunt end. It was easy to detect the power and grace of the creature even as it went through its cleaning performance. The muscles of the neck and shoulders rippled beneath its skin as it used its paws, feline fashion, to wipe its face; then it licked its coat, patch by patch, with loose, easy motions of the head. The animal's confidence in its own supremacy amounted to arrogance as it turned a disdainful glance on its audience. The motley collection of onlookers was, quite simply, overwhelmed. They had never seen such a beast before. They were overwhelmed by its size, by its majestic ease, and by a consciousness that it could scatter the whole pack of them if it should choose to do so. But they did not disperse. They were held by a fascination for the creature's beauty. To them it was perfection – a being from a strange world they did not know. They were lost in their admiration for it.

None of these lesser creatures could break the spell. That was left to the great Cat itself. When it was satisfied its coat was clean, it bent to take a few laps from the stream. Then, with a final glance in their direction that seemed to imply a sort of challenge, the Cat leapt into the water, dashing spray everywhere. In a few moments it had reached the opposite bank and, with a series of effortless bounds, it was away and lost from sight before the animals could draw breath.

But the spell was broken and all of the onlookers began to cry out to each other. Only then did they remember their purpose.

Whisper said to Fox, 'The Beast is huge – I think as big as a great mastiff dog that befriended Bold and myself. But this Cat is no friend. It's an enemy and an enemy we are powerless to stop.'

—12—

Thralldom

It was not long before the smaller and weaker animals disbanded. They did not even wait for their leader, Fox, to give them new directions. They had seen all they wanted to see. As far as they could tell, Fox was helpless, and they themselves were keen to get out of the unnaturally vulnerable position in which they were situated. Predators were on all sides.

The larger animals and the hunters among the group began to complain that they had come to do something and now the opportunity had been missed. They spoke from the safe knowledge that the Cat was no longer near.

The birds flew away. Their limited interest in the venture had soon been dissipated. Only Tawny Owl had the presence of mind to follow the Cat as far as he could.

Fox was silent. He knew his plan was a failure and he thought that probably it had been doomed from the outset. But he had felt a need to be doing *something* and so the expedition had been mounted. Now the Park's inhabitants would no longer believe he had any right to expect them to follow him. He had shown that he was as inadequate in dealing with the Cat as any of them.

Vixen watched him. She could guess much of what was in his heart. 'At least you tried,' she murmured to him.

'Tried!' he growled. 'The Beast showed its contempt for all of us. The entire Reserve is in thralldom.'

She tried to comfort him. 'We mustn't forget the skilfulness of Man,' she reminded him. 'There's always a chance the Warden will catch up with it.'

'Perhaps,' Fox said morosely. 'Anyway, that's our only hope now.'

The larger animals were gradually drifting away. Most of them were relieved that they had not actually had to prove themselves in a confrontation. As it was, they were not unduly pessimistic about the situation. They felt that, now the deer herd was in the open again, the rest of them would only be secondary targets. In the end only the Farthing Wood contingent remained.

'Did you find another entrance to the lair?' Toad asked Fox lamely.

'No. But there could be other bolt-holes all over the park, and what difference would it make?' Fox sounded bitter.

'We – we seemed to be hypnotized,' stammered Mossy. He was so purblind that he had not seen the Cat himself, but he understood the reaction.

'Exactly,' Badger corroborated. 'I found myself marvelling at the creature. I've lived a long time and seen all sorts of things, but never anything quite like that.'

The vixens were eager to get back to their dens and their cubs. It was only Fox the elder's call for solidarity that had induced them to leave them. So the numbers of animals dwindled bit by bit until only a handful were left, staring disconsolately across the water to where the Cat had vanished from sight.

'We don't seem to be achieving much by staying here,' Adder drawled, 'so I think I'll just slip away.'

None of the others attempted to stop him. Mossy was heartily glad to see the back of the snake. He was not sure that Adder was party to the conspiracy about 'Mole'. Toad alone called a farewell.

'I don't expect Tawny Owl will have achieved much either,' Weasel remarked. But his observation was not quite accurate.

There was a stretch of open land on the far side of the stream and Tawny Owl was able to keep the Cat in view quite well, though he could not match its pace. It moved very swiftly, with a bounding movement of its long legs. Owl realized it was heading directly for the Park's boundary but, surprisingly, on the side where it bordered a lane leading to human habitations. Eventually the Cat was lost among the first belt of trees. Tawny Owl flew on faithfully in its wake.

A ditch ran along the edge of the Park, just beyond the perimeter fence. Hazel bushes and young trees hung over it from the Park side. At one point under the fence animals had dug the soil away and there was a gap. The Cat knew about this, and it knew about the ditch. It had crossed a large chunk of the Reserve in broad daylight and now arrived at the boundary. It flattened its back and scrambled under the fence, then jumped down into the ditch. This channel was for drainage but it had not been cleared since the previous summer. Leaves and twigs had accumulated in it from the overhanging boughs, so much of it was reasonably dry. The Cat squatted in the bottom. Sunlight pierced the greenery irregularly, dappling the ground all about. The Cat's markings blended in perfectly with its surroundings. From the road it was hidden. No human stroller passing by would have noticed, nor suspected, the existence of a large beast skulking in the ditch. The Cat made sure its head was well out of sight. It had discovered that this spot was a good place to lie in wait for any prey that might wander in the trees. It had caught squirrels and rabbits here and once, in the evening, a deer had stepped almost close enough for a pounce. The Cat could see animals walking along the road too. It was not averse to the possibility of leaping out at an unaccompanied dog.

Tawny Owl reached this edge of the Reserve a minute or so after the Cat had hidden itself. He flew along the Park's perimeter, always searching for a sign of that tawny coat. He actually perched in a branch that overlooked the ditch, but the Cat's splendid camouflage fooled him for a while. Then the slightest of movements caught his roving eye. His head swivelled round and he stared long and hard. All was still. Was he imagining things? No, there it was again. Just a twitch of the back fur. A midge or spider had caused a moment's irritation. Now Owl could make out the long powerful body. What was it doing in the ditch? It certainly could not know it was being observed. Owl decided to move even closer.

He looked round and selected a stout sycamore sapling that grew right on the edge of the drainage channel. He fluttered over to it and alighted. It was not the best of landings. The sapling bent under his weight and he grappled for a firmer hold. The sycamore's leaves shook noticeably. The Cat turned sharply and looked directly at Tawny Owl. Its lips curled back in a soundless snarl, annoyed that it had been detected. This time Owl maintained his position, aware that he was out of reach, and stared back full in the Beast's face. The Cat's eyes did not waver and in the end it was Tawny Owl who looked away. But there was a magnetism about the Cat and it drew the bird's head round again. The Beast opened its mouth.

'I am of interest to you?' Its voice was strange, like a combination of a roar and a howl. It was a very strong voice and quite an alarming one. But although it spoke loudly and slowly, Tawny Owl had difficulty in understanding. This was partly due to his fright at the sound and partly due to the unexpectedness of it. He had never heard an animal cry of this kind before. He slipped a little on the sapling but quickly strengthened his grip.

'I – I'm afraid I didn't – er – follow that,' he fluted nervously.

In a grating sort of growl the Cat said, 'You have pursued me. You have much interest in me.'

Tawny Owl strained his ears and was able to catch the gist of the remarks.

'I'm certainly interested,' he replied. 'You're of interest to all of us.' He was very aware of his role as the mouthpiece of White Deer Park. 'Yes, I followed you. We need to know where you are.'

The Cat appeared to have no difficulty in understanding Owl and it snarled softly as he finished speaking. It did not like the idea of its movements being noted. 'You do not need to know,' it growled threateningly. 'Owls do not tempt my appetite. But you should not mistake. Trees are my playthings. I can stalk you.'

Tawny Owl marked the warning. Yet he realized the creature assumed he was speaking only for his own kind.

'The inhabitants of this Park,' he went on, 'are terrified of you. You arrived from we know not where with great suddenness – a frightening alien. Our humble little world has been rent apart. If we don't know where you are or when you might pounce, how can the animals guard their own safety?'

It was a foolish thing to say to a hunter and Tawny Owl soon perceived this when he saw a wicked feline grin spread slowly across the Cat's face.

'The secret of my success,' it acknowledged with a harsh sort of purr.

'No doubt,' remarked Tawny Owl. He had lost his unease and was beginning to enjoy himself. He anticipated what a celebrity he was to become – the first to hold a conversation with the great hunter! 'Your stealth,' he continued, 'is legendary amongst us. We respect your expertise and the way you even manage to evade the humans. But – '

The Cat interrupted him with a mocking roar. 'Humans!' it scoffed, growling. 'What do they know of my kind; our ancient lineage? They know nothing of our existence. We have roamed the land for longer than they. Never have they captured us, nor even seen enough to know what we are. We are survivors of the Old Animal Lore. How can they hope to comprehend? They think they are Masters. We know *no* Masters.'

Tawny Owl was rather taken aback by this mysterious speech, and did not himself understand much of it. In his familiar limited world Man was always evident. How could humans not know about the Cat and the rest of its kind? He was so puzzled he had to ask about it.

'Do you mean you have never been detected by Man at all?' he blurted out incredulously.

'Never,' roared the Cat with a sort of defiance. 'And so it will be. There are more creatures prowling their domains than *he* knows of.'

Tawny Owl was silent as he tried to digest the facts, which seemed to him almost unbelievable. He had to remind himself that none of the Park's animal population had ever seen such a Beast before. But humans were quite different – they were so clever, so wise, so all-knowing . . . . He tried to bring himself back to the subject in hand, but first he could not resist risking a gibe.

'I shouldn't roar quite so much,' he hooted with mock innocence, 'if you want to retain your history of secrecy.'

The Beast gave him such a withering look of contempt that Tawny Owl at once regretted the remark. He said hastily, 'Will you stay here long? Er – couldn't you perhaps hunt somewhere else?'

'Where I hunt is no concern of an owl,' the Cat rasped.

'But – but – you see,' Tawny Owl stuttered, 'we're all together in this. Er – I mean, we're all afraid and we feel while you remain in the Reserve we – er – we remain at risk. Er – all of us.'

The Cat flattened itself in the ditch bottom as a car approached along the road. When this had passed and its noise entirely disappeared, the animal said gruffly, 'I have told you. I do not prey on owls.' Then it added menacingly, 'Unless they try to meddle . . . .'

Tawny Owl knew it was hopeless. It was no use his endeavouring to explain that he was speaking for the whole community. The Cat would never understand they had a common interest in ridding their home of its threat. Nor could it ever appreciate how Owl and his closest friends were bound by the Farthing Wood Oath to help and act for each other. It belonged to a separate sort of existence altogether.

The Cat half pulled itself out of the ditch. Tawny Owl flew quickly to a higher point.

'You have been lucky,' the Cat told him. 'I made no special effort to avoid you. But I give you my word. You will go now and, after your departure, you will not see me again; not you nor any creature that ranges this area. *Though I shall still be here.* If I am wrong about this you shall have your wish. I shall leave for fresh terrain and never return, if any one of you, beast or bird, sets eyes on me and tells me so. Now go.'

With dumb obedience Tawny Owl took a last look at the strange beast and then flew away. He did not stop until he had arrived at one of his home perches. He pondered over the Cat's peculiar offer. Was it a challenge? Did it intend some amusement for itself, by giving such an exhibition of cunning and stealth to them all that it would exceed even that which had impressed them already? There was no telling what was in its mind. But Tawny Owl believed its word. To his way of thinking, they all had an incentive now. It only needed one sighting, by perhaps the lowliest of the Park's population, for the Cat's sway to end. So let the whole of White deer Park become like a thousand eyes looking inward, in a perpetual examination of every leaf, every twig, every blade of grass. Soon, surely, in this way the state of siege would be lifted.

—13—
The Pledge

Tawny Owl hastened to the side of the stream. When he had left it earlier, most of the population of the Reserve had been gathered there. Now it was deserted. Every bird, every beast, every reptile and amphibian had disappeared, just as if the assemblage had never existed. They had retreated like a defeated army. Tawny Owl saw it as the greatest demonstration of the Cat's power. It had won a complete victory without needing to deliver a blow.

Upstream a lone heron was fishing. Whistler had returned to his normal activities, almost as if he had never been interrupted. As Owl spotted him the tall bird bent his long neck and then stabbed down with his beak into the water. When he raised it again it contained a wriggling silver fish which was swallowed at a gulp. The entire sequence lasted but a few seconds.

'*He's* busy,' said Tawny Owl to himself. He was full of his conversation with the Cat and wanted to tell everyone. But he was also very weary and decided he would only do his tale full justice by relating it when he was more alert. He must get across to his friends the significance of the strange pledge the Cat had made. So he avoided the heron and returned to his roost. Daylight, he reflected, was definitely not the time when owls were at their best.

Dusk passed Tawny Owl by. The evening wore on and still he slept. So the warning that might have been carried sooner to the deer herd to be extra vigilant was too late to save another fawn. While Tawny Owl slumbered on, the Cat had ample time to select its victim, trail it and strike, first at the mother, then at her baby. Neither had an inkling that the predator was around. The hind was left where it had been killed. The young and tender fawn was carried off, limp and lifeless. The Cat was hidden again long before the deaths were discovered. But not in the ditch. That was abandoned. The owl would be the only creature to see the Beast there.

During the night Tawny Owl awoke. He rustled his wings sleepily without at first remembering any more than that the was in his own comfortable roost in the hollow tree. Then he remembered he was hungry. He was surprised to find he had left a couple of mice uneaten. He soon remedied that.

Whilst he was eating he thought he heard a voice calling him from somewhere in the tree. Owl was still dozy and could not at first make out where it was coming from. Then he saw Squirrel skipping down towards him from a high branch.

'We've all been wondering if you found out anything,' said the quicksilver creature, flicking his bushy tail restlessly.

Now Tawny Owl recalled his message and tried to hoot through the middle of a mouthful, nearly choking himself in the process. He swallowed elaborately.

'Yes, yes,' he spluttered. 'Most urgent. Glad you came, Squirrel. I've *spoken* to the Cat. It made a kind of bargain.'

Squirrel was showing his amazement by flicking his tail harder than ever. He sat on his hind legs one moment and then ran up a branch and back again the next moment, unable to keep still. 'The Beast *spoke*?' he chattered.

'More of a roar, really. A horrible sound,' Tawny Owl told him. 'But come with me, Squirrel. I must tell Fox and the rest.' He flew noiselessly away and Squirrel followed him, racing and leaping through the tree-tops.

It was some time before Tawny Owl managed to bring together Fox, Vixen, Weasel and Badger. He recounted his story with the exaggerations and embellishments that, by now, were expected of him. But his message was clear.

'We have a real chance this time,' he asserted. 'The whole Park was on watch before. But we must try harder this time. Our lives depend on it.'

'I'll talk to the Great Stag,' said Fox at once. 'The herd must be involved this time. They have to be especially wakeful. If the Beast wants a sort of contest of skills we'll give it one. Our eyes against his stealth.'

'That's what it will mean,' Tawny Owl averred.

'You did well to follow him,' Weasel congratulated the bird unexpectedly. 'Toad got close, but you alone have conversed with the Cat.'

Tawny Owl swelled visibly with pride. However there was no time for self-congratulation.

'We have a cause again,' Vixen remarked. 'Our future safety depends on us now – not just on our little band, but on every other one of the Park's inhabitants too. Even the smallest newt or fledgling has a stake in this, if it only needs one sighting for our home to return to its natural state.'

'Proof of a sighting,' Tawny Owl corrected her. 'And I'm afraid, as far as I understand, newts are dumb.'

'All right, Owl, I extended the list too far. But you told us – any creature, big or small, would serve the same purpose.'

'As far as I'm concerned,' said Fox, 'if I thought I could bring about our salvation I'd stay awake day and night till I found the brute.'

'And I too,' Badger wheezed. 'It would be one last useful achievement before I – '

'Now, Badger,' Weasel cut in. 'Don't start talking in that vein again. There's no question of it being a last anything, we hope. Think of Mo – er – Mole.'

'Oh yes. Poor Mole. How empty my tunnels would seem for him if I weren't around.'

'Well, then,' said Fox, 'shall we begin? We have to pass the word again. If we thought we searched and watched hard before, now we have a real test before us. I shall go straight to the deer herd.' He left and the group hurriedly broke up.

On his way across the Reserve towards the open area where the bulk of the white deer herd was usually found,

Fox fell in with Friendly. The younger animal confessed to his father that he had feelings of guilt about Husky's death.

'You weren't entirely to blame,' Fox told him. 'It was a rash adventure, but the reasons for which it was undertaken are commendable.'

'I feel I led him on – and the other youngsters,' Friendly went on. 'I shouldn't have pressed them into it.'

'I think none of us have really understood what we are up against,' Fox remarked generously. 'Now I think we're closer to it, after what we all saw by the stream. What were my empty words worth, about protecting and avenging our own? Dreams, Friendly, no more. We're out of our depth. I've felt myself to be weak and helpless as never before.'

Friendly looked at his father – the greying coat, the stiffer gait, the duller eye. Age was the great enemy, he thought. But Fox knew what was in his mind and denied it.

'Were I your age again,' he said, 'it would make no difference. I'd have no challenge to make to monsters.'

'Let's be thankful, then,' said Friendly, 'that we have some skills.'

'Yes,' conceded his father. 'At least we have our eyes.'

They went on together, feeling that they had helped to raise each other's spirits.

The Great White Stag saw them approaching, shoulder to shoulder, through the swift-growing grasses. He had the news of the killings ready for them.

'I am indeed sorry,' Fox responded afterwards. 'You have lost quite a few of this season's young?'

'Too many,' the Stag boomed in his deep voice. 'Fox, we appeal to you. You have been our friend since you came to our home. We deer have lived here, mostly at peace, for generations. But we cannot sustain these losses indefinitely. How do we fight back?'

'By the summer your antlers will have grown again,' Fox said. 'They are potent weapons. But it may not be necessary to wait for that. There is another weapon we all possess, Man and ourselves. Vision. And the hunter himself has told us how we can use it.' He went on to explain the Beast's pledge. 'Watchfulness,' he finished, 'from dawn to dusk and through the night. That's the only hope for any of us.'

'We have watched,' replied the leader of the herd. 'And when we were enclosed, the men watched for us. But still it was of no use.'

'We *must* have a chance,' Fox declared, 'and we must believe that we have it. The Cat is not invisible. We have to remember that.'

'We shall try,' the Stag said unhappily. 'What else can we do?' He began to walk away in his sedate manner. Then he turned back. 'Last time it killed my favourite hind,' he bemoaned. 'She had borne many young.' He looked away and murmured, 'It has such contempt for us all.'

His words were uncannily accurate. Even as they spoke, the Cat returned to drag away the hind's carcass. It meant to ensure that its larder was well stocked.

So word travelled round the Park again. Tawny Owl and Whistler spread it amongst the birds who were the best carriers of messages, and the beasts played their part too. Soon all were aware that they now had a real hope of banishing the threat from their lives by their own efforts.

Meanwhile the Warden was taking stock too. The morning after the kill he went to take count of the deer herd as he did every morning. He was paricularly concerned about the survival of the young, and he quickly noticed another was missing. He knew the hinds too; each one that had given birth that season. So he realized the mother had been taken as well.

The next day Vixen's words were borne out. A party of men began a systematic search of White Deer Park. Some were on horseback, some on foot. Many were armed. Others had brought apparatus for capturing the Beast. The search lasted throughout the day. The whole of the Reserve was combed. No trace of the hunter was found.

The other animals in the Park kept themselves out of sight, too, whilst the men roamed around. The more intelligent ones guessed what was going on, and hoped fervently that the Cat would be discovered and removed by human hand. But they heard no report of guns and the birds noted that the men went away empty-handed. Tawny Owl recalled the Cat's words and was not surprised. However, the men had not finished. They were about to use new tactics.

The day after the search they returned. Under the leadership of the Warden traps were laid at various points throughout the Reserve and baited with fresh raw meat. The Warden had taken the utmost care to ensure that these traps could only be sprung by a large and very powerful animal – the huge chunks of meat were set in such a way that no fox or smaller carnivore would have the strength to dislodge them. The men retired again and then the waiting began. The Warden reckoned that the hunter probably had sufficient food for itself for quite some time.

The days went by. The Cat went nowhere near any of the traps. Each day the Warden went to inspect them, sometimes by himself, and sometimes with a helper. The meat was renewed at intervals. At night many of the smaller animals had investigated these unusual food sources. The foxes had been suspicious and only sniffed at them. Some of the smaller meat-eaters had tried to pull the lumps away, failed, and then contended themselves with nibbling at them where they were.

After some time both the Warden and his charges began to think that the Beast had decided it had nothing to gain by staying around that part of the world any longer. For not only had the traps been avoided, but no further deer had been taken. Indeed no smaller prey had been attacked either.

'I'm beginning to wonder about this "pledge" of the Cat's,' Weasel commented one day to Fox. 'How do we know it isn't a final trick on us – you know, to put us all on our guard for nothing, while he himself is as far away as – as – '

'Farthing Wood?' suggested Fox wryly.

'Precisely!'

'Yes, I've thought of that too,' Fox admitted. 'But don't tell Owl. He'll think you're doubting his word.'

'I know, I know,' said Weasel. 'But what would that matter by comparison with the benefit to us all? To be sure that White Deer Park is ours again!'

' "To be sure",' Fox echoed. 'That's the crux of it, Weasel. How can we ever be sure again?'

Weasel looked crestfallen. 'I hadn't thought of it like that,' he muttered. 'I suppose it would be preferable for one of us to see the great hunter again.'

But nobody did. And, understandably, the animals' wariness began to slacken and their watchfulness to be relaxed. They no longer believed they were watching for any purpose. As for the Warden, he did not bother to replace the bait in his traps any more. Replenishing the meat was costly and it was all to no avail. Besides which, he had still a lingering doubt about the risks involved – perhaps one of the traps might catch an animal that actually had a perfect right to be in the Reserve. After a few more days and much cogitation, the Warden at last decided to remove the traps altogether. So the guard was down of animal and human alike. And that was exactly what the Cat had been waiting for.

It had eaten well at the beginning. The fawn and its mother provided plenty of meat. Eventually every scrap of the carcasses was gone, leaving only skeletons. The Cat even crunched some of the bones. It had managed to lap at the dew and take rainwater from the plentiful showers, so that thirst had been no problem for it. As time passed, hunger returned, but it knew it would not have long to wait, and it was content. It had found itself an underground home which served its need for secrecy and stealth perfectly. It waited with patience for its great cunning to work its effect.

Then one dusk the Beast knew that the time was right. It waited for the true darkness that came late at that period of the year. Then it crept forth from its den and embarked on a small orgy of slaughter, prompted by its long fast. It killed rabbits and hares and any small creatures it could find on the ground. Voles and frogs were snapped up at a gulp. Then it climbed into the trees and caught birds on their nests and squirrels in their dreys. Those creatures that were not eaten at once were carried back to the den for future use. But it did not approach the deer herd. It was too clever for that.

Leveret missed being taken by a whisker. The instinctive leap that took him to safety exposed his mate and she was taken instead. Leveret ran at full tilt through the grass. His electrifying pace could outdistance almost any creature. He did not stop to see if he was pursued. So he did not see the Cat. He kept right on running until he ran into Badger, nearly bowling him over.

'Leveret!' Badger gasped, badly winded. 'What's the alarm?'

The hare explained at once about the attack. Neither of them could be sure whether it was the Cat at work again, but they both jumped to conclusions.

'And we thought it had gone,' Badger murmured. 'It's been playing with us.'

'Well, it's not playing now,' Leveret said harshly.

Their suspicions were justified. Knowledge soon spread of the killings. There seemed to be a new savagery about these, as if the Cat had a lust to kill for the sake of it, to demonstrate its mastery over the rest of them.

No animal, no bird had seen it. But all of the Park soon knew the stranger was still around. There was only one clue that impressed itself on the more intelligent of the population. The slaughter had been confined to one corner of the Reserve. And that was the corner where the animals from Farthing Wood had established their homes.

'Can it be deliberate?' they asked each other.

'Is it hiding nearby?'

Squirrel was terrified and planned to move his home. Leveret discovered the loss of his mate and no longer cared if the hunter should return. Fox and Vixen racked their brains as to the whereabouts of the Beast. After such killings, how could it just vanish again? Tawny Owl perched in his tree and hoped no one would come near him. He had the awful feeling that in some way he was to blame for this: that the Cat meant to prove something to him. He was to be punished for his previous presumption, not personally perhaps, but through the deaths of his friends.

—14—
Hearts and Minds

The animal friends waited for the next strike with a fear that had become all-consuming. They scarcely dared to go about their necessary activities. The collection of food was now a hurried, furtive business – something to be done as quickly as possible before scurrying back to cower at home. Only the birds, Adder and Toad felt comparatively secure. Adder had not been seen for a while, but the others worried daily about the safety of their companions. Tawny Owl, in particular, was in a state of unending misery. He could not bring himself to talk to anyone. He had started to think that, if he did, that animal would be the next one singled out for the Cat's attention.

Friendly wanted to make one last attempt to go on the offensive. His mate, Russet, was terrified for her growing cubs, who had now reached the stage of wanting to explore farther than around their parent's earth. Other vixens, Charmer and Whisper, were in the same situation. Friendly thought they could not continue to live their lives under threat. He suggested to his father that the only way to break the dreadful monotony was to sniff out the blood trail once more, and follow it to the Cat's hideout.

'There would be no fighting,' he assured his father. 'It would just need one of us to go close enough to *see*.'

'I understand how you feel,' said Fox. 'But it's far too dangerous. Probably the Beast is waiting for just such a foolhardy creature as you to come along. What would another death achieve?'

'There will be deaths anyway,' said Friendly. 'Why skulk here where the hunter can pounce as it chooses? *I'm* willing to take the risk. I ask for no supporters.'

Fox admired his courage, not for the first time. 'Wait a while yet, Friendly,' he pleaded. 'I have a feeling the Cat might make a slip, and it only needs one.'

'What if it decides not to honour this wonderful pledge Owl talks about?' Friendly growled. 'There would be nothing any of us could do about it.'

'Then why do you wish to track it?' Fox asked at once.

Friendly had tripped himself up and knew it. He looked glum. 'All right,' he conceded. 'I'll do as you say. But I hope it won't result in suffering for my cubs.'

Since the gathering by the stream, Adder had had something else on his mind besides the Cat – something very private. It was a she-viper that occupied his mind, a female adder with a bold disposition and a coolness of temperament that matched his own. Whilst he wondered why she was in his thoughts, he constantly asked himself whether he was in hers. There was no doubt that, if Adder had been more familiar with such things, he would have realized that he wanted her company.

Of course, he would never have deliberately sought her out. But it was strange how he found himself, without intention, returning to the places where he had seen her before. She was not in any of them. It was hardly likely she would have been, he told himself. Why should she stay around there? So it must have been coincidence that prompted their next meeting.

Adder had caught and eaten two wood mice amongst the grasses. He was no longer hungry now, but his hunting instincts had not subsided and he was still very much alert. He caught the soft rustling of a creature moving through the stems close to the ground. He prepared himself to ambush another mouse. But, as the mouse came into view, with its nose quivering incessantly, another snake shot from hiding and seized it. Adder watched with feigned indifference as the plump little morsel went down another throat. The she-viper, in the ecstatic throes of a series of swallows, had not yet noticed him. However, when the last muscular ripple had passed along her body, she became aware of his presence.

'The solitude-lover,' she remarked, as if to herself. 'I'd better not stay here too long and risk complaint.'

'It's not necessary for you to move just yet,' Adder answered quickly. (He thought this sounded like someone else talking.) 'Er – have you caught many mice?'

'Very many,' she quipped. 'One gets through quite a lot in a season.'

'You know I didn't mean that,' he lisped with a mild sense of irritation. 'Are you always so clever?'

'Only when I have the opportunity,' she told him coolly. Her face was as expressionless as ever. 'Are you still looking for the Cat?' she asked next.

'I? *I'm* not looking,' Adder declared, as if the idea of his putting himself out was quite absurd.

'But I thought the plan was for every creature to keep its eyes open?'

'Oh, my eyes are open,' he responded, 'but I'm not – er – looking . . . .' (How silly that sounded.)

The she-viper refrained from comment but she stared at him. So Adder stared back. At last she said: 'You're looking fatter than when I saw you before.'

'Frogs, insects and mice,' he explained succinctly.

'I though the adder that came here from a distant place wasn't supposed to eat mammals?' she went on.

'I didn't know you knew who I was,' he answered.

'The shortness of your tail gives you away.'

'I see. Well, if you're referring to that ridiculous Oath I was made to swear before I was allowed to travel here with the others, it only forbade *certain* mice and voles from my diet. Those being, of course, the ones from my old home.'

'How do you tell them apart?'

'Oh, they're all dead now. They live lives of extra-ordinary brevity. Of course I left them alone while they did live. But they've produced so many generations since we arrived here that I can't tell the difference any more.'

'So what do you do?'

'Eat whenever I feel like it,' he declared. 'As far as I'm concerned that Oath doesn't stretch into infinity.'

'Very wise of you,' the she-viper remarked. 'The whole thing is difficult to understand – how you consort with mammals at all.'

Adder was in a quandary. He never liked to admit he

owed obligations to any creature. Yet there still remained a select few for whom, and with whom, he felt bound. Fox and Vixen, Badger, Toad and – yes, he supposed Tawny Owl and Weasel. All of them were bound irrevocably and for ever. But he was not going to tell the she-viper.

'I don't seek them out,' he said truthfully. 'But, you see, there is an old association.' That was as far as he would go.

The she-viper's next words startled him with their implication. 'How would you feel about a new association?'

How was he to take this? Was she suggesting . . . ?

'I'm not entirely sure . . . .' he began guardedly.

'Oh yes, Adder. You're quite sure,' she drawled with a certain amount of ironic humour. 'You're the lover of solitude.'

Now that he was being branded with this description, Adder was not completely happy to own it. There had been moments, he recalled, when he . . . . When he what? he asked himself. He did not know if he could bring himself to admit that he had hoped for company at times. And then again, *whose* company? Oh, he was in a rare old muddle.

'I do like solitude,' he hissed uncertainly. 'But I suppose how much I like it is governed by how much of it I get.' (What did that convey? he wondered. Had he given something away?)

'And that depends on how much of it you seek,' she returned. She was determined to put him on the spot and was relishing every moment.

'Well, yes, that would appear to be the case,' Adder said. (Wherever would all of this end? He was almost beginning to feel uncomfortable.)

'You can call me Sinuous,' she offered.

'Can I? Is that how you're known?'

'It's how I'd like to be known by you.'

Adder wanted to get away. He was not competent to deal with situations of this kind. But he could not put his body into motion.

'It's very warm,' said Sinuous. 'If you've eaten enough it would be a good time to bask.'

The invitation was obvious. Adder felt he was powerless to resist. He made no answer. Sinuous took this as a sign of agreement and began to slither away through the grass stalks. Adder followed her mechanically.

The she-viper led him to a small depression in the ground where the grass had been flattened by a larger animal. It felt dry and hot. Adder wondered fleetingly what creature had been lying there before.

'I like this spot,' commented Sinuous. 'It's well hidden.'

'It seems that another has found it favourable too,' Adder remarked.

'Yes, I saw him once or twice before I started using it,' she answered.

'Saw him? Whom?'

'The Cat.'

'The Cat! Does he still come here?' Adder hissed urgently.

'Oh no. He's disappeared, hasn't he?' Sinuous sounded uninterested. She was coiling herself up.

Adder was irritated. 'You're very secretive,' he told her. 'If we'd known this earlier, it might have saved – '

'It wouldn't have saved anything,' she interrupted. 'I know the terms of the Beast's so-called pledge and, since then, I've naturally kept a look-out here. But, of course, I don't expect to see anything now.'

'I see,' said Adder. 'No, it's not likely to return to any of its old haunts. It must know this whole Reserve better than any of us. Yet I still don't understand how it can remain in the Park and stay concealed.'

'Supposing it is not *in* the Park but under it?' Sinuous suggested nonchalantly. 'Perhaps that's the answer.' She seemed to want to finish with the subject and enjoy her sunbath. But the remark had the very opposite effect on Adder.

'Underground,' he hissed. 'Yesss.' All thought of repose left him. 'That's where it must be.'

Sinuous paid no attention. Adder could only think of those of his old companions who made their homes underground, and who might be able to make use of this theory. Fox and Vixen, Badger and Weasel sprang immediately to mind. It was a pity Mole, that champion tunneller, was no longer with them. But then Adder recalled something about one of Mole's kin who had come into the picture recently. The relationship escaped him.

'My basking will have to be postponed,' he informed Sinuous. 'This idea can't be kept to ourselves.'

'Ah – the old association,' Sinuous murmured. 'Well, you must go to your warm-blooded friends.'

'I must. But – er – well, I shall remember this place,' said Adder. He was unable to make more of a commitment than that. He slid away.

'Only the place?' Sinuous asked him. But Adder's hearing was not good.

He went first of all to Badger.

It was broad daylight and the old animal's snoring seemed to reverberate through his network of tunnels as Adder entered the set. The snake was glad of this, for the pitch darkness engulfed him almost at once, but he was able to guide himself to Badger's sleeping chamber by the sound. Badger was not easily woken. He slept deeply and Adder's lisping voice was not the most resonant.

The snake became more and more aggravated as his efforts to rouse the sleeper continued to fail. He considered whether he should risk a nip at the thickest part of Badger's coat, where his dangerous fangs would be very unlikely to penetrate the skin. Luckily such a gamble did not prove necessary. Badger stirred.

'At last!' Adder hissed. 'I've been here for an eternity.'

Badger quickly roused himself. 'Adder? Whatever are you – '

'No time for that,' the snake answered shortly. 'I need your advice. Listen.' He explained the theory of the she-viper without mentioning her.

'Oh no. That's not likely. I've already rejected the idea,' Badger informed him. 'There's no set or earth around here big enough to take that huge beast.'

'Who said anything about around here?' Adder queried impatiently. 'In the length and breadth of the Reserve there might be many holes it could hide itself in.'

'No,' Badger insisted. 'I would know about it. And if *I* didn't, it would be known by the foxes or the rabbits or the weasels or – or – the moles. Besides which, Adder, we know the Cat *is* in our neck of the woods.'

'Just because it hunted around here doesn't mean it hides around here,' Adder argued. 'Not all the time.'

'Well, Squirrel is convinced of it. He's taken his family and set up home in another quarter.'

'Squirrel is not the most knowledgeable of the community,' Adder drawled. 'I feel it would be worthwhile for all the foxes and animals like yourself, and maybe the rabbits, to be consulted. They may know of a likely den.'

'I'll ask Mole when I see him,' Badger said. 'He's the greatest digger of us all.'

'Don't be absurd, Badger,' Adder rasped. 'Your memory is playing you tricks again.'

'Oh no,' Badger contradicted him. 'You're mistaken. I often talk to him.'

Adder thought it was futile to continue this line of conversation, so he told Badger he was going to pay a visit on Fox and then leave everything to him. The cold and dark of Badger's set made him wish he had not left the warm sunny spot where Sinuous was now lying.

'Wait,' said Badger. 'I'll come with you.'

'No need,' the snake told him. Then he added unkindly, 'You'd better stay here in case Mole decides to make one of his miraculous returns.'

Fox responded in the same way to the underground theory. But he agreed to talk to all his relatives to see if they might know of a large hideout under the Park.

'It's more than possible,' Adder pointed out. 'You didn't know of the existence of the lair by the stream until I told you of it.'

'You're right, Adder,' Fox said. 'But where did *you* learn of it? You never did say definitely. Perhaps from the same source as this latest idea?'

Adder never had any difficulty in retaining his equanimity. His natural expression was one of immobility. His ceaselessly flickering tongue was the only sign of movement from his face.

'The source isn't important,' he replied enigmatically.

Fox knew he would not be permitted to pry any further. So he said, 'Have you spoken to Mossy?'

Adder searched his memory. 'Mossy?' he muttered.

Fox reminded him.

'A descendant of Mole? Well, it's likely that Badger will see him first then. Who knows – perhaps this Mossy will be in the company of his forefather!'

'I'm glad Badger's not around to hear that,' said Fox. 'Poor old creature, he's never been able to accept the loss of Mole. This game he plays is the only way he can come to terms with it.'

'I wish you'd explain, Fox. Badger was rambling on about Mole when I spoke to him just now. I think he must have been still half-asleep.'

'On no, it's quite deliberate. I thought you knew about it. The rest of us take part.' He told Adder about Mossy's role.

'Now I comprehend,' said the snake. 'But I certainly don't approve. I'm surprised at you all, making such fools of yourselves.'

'You sound just like Owl,' Fox remarked. 'Think of Badger. Haven't you any heart?'

'I shouldn't be talking to you now if I hadn't. But perhaps the reptilian variety hasn't the same capacity as a mammal's for spreading warmth.'

'Perhaps.'

'Don't worry, I shan't upset anything of your "game". And now I'll leave you to your subterranean explorations. I'm for a warmer place. Who knows' – and now Adder was talking to himself as much as to Fox – 'perhaps my heart will benefit from it.'

—15—
Mossy's Mission

Fox and Vixen discussed the underground theory with their kindred. Friendly and Russet, Charmer and Ranger, Whisper, Pace and Rusty had no knowledge that was of any use. Ranger volunteered to consult Trip and the other foxes in the Park. Meanwhile Weasel talked to his own kind whilst Leveret spoke to his cousins the rabbits. All of the inquiries drew a blank. Then the other badgers in the Reserve were brought in. All of them were of the opinion that none of the sets they knew about had entrances or tunnels wide enough to admit a creature the size of the Cat.

The Cat itself, since its last hunting spree, was lying low

in more than one sense. But it was about to replenish its stores of food. At the time when its hunger dictated, it emerged from its new lair. The night was dark. There was no moon, and clouds completely obscured the heavens. The Cat was well aware the animals expected another strike in the same neighbourhood. So it avoided that and slunk through the shadows on its noiseless way towards the stream. But not to where the stream ran past its old lair in the bank. Another lower reach of the water was its objective.

The Cat was a good swimmer and it decided now to explore the food potential not only of the banks, but of the water itself. It caught a couple of unsuspecting water-voles, hooked out some small fish, and completely obliterated a family of coots on their midstream nest. But it was not satisfied. It was disappointed in this aquatic hunt, and a few frogs made very little difference to its appetite. As the sky began to lighten, the Cat loped back towards its den, determined to snatch itself something more substantial on the way.

The Reserve seemed deserted. The animals were still spending most of their time out of sight. The Cat stopped dead, thinking of the taste of deer flesh. Its mouth watered. But it was too late now. The first signs of dawn were in the sky. It padded back, angry and frustrated, to its den. The next night it meant to eat deer again. At the entrace to its lair it roared its anger to the cowering inhabitants of the Park. The roar rose in pitch and finished in an unearthly scream that carried far beyond the boundaries of the Reserve. The Warden of White Deer Park woke in his bed, dressed hurriedly, snatched his gun and a torch and ran from the house. He stayed near the deer herd until broad day, but he saw nothing.

That night Mossy had decided to travel one of his tunnels that led into Badger's set. It was a passage that had been often trodden by his father. He began to call to Badger in between snacks of earthworms which he collected as he went along. Badger did not reply, so Mossy settled down for a proper feast. Eating was such an absorbing pastime for a mole that, by the time he dropped into the set, Mossy had no idea it was nearly daybreak.

Badger had returnd from a half-hearted foraging trip and was preparing himself for a snooze. But when Mossy appeared, he was delighted to postpone it.

'Mole! Just the fellow I've been thinking about,' was the greeting. 'Adder came to see me and – you won't guess! – he has the idea that the Cat is living underground like us.'

Mossy gave a cry of alarm but Badger soon reassured him.

'It's all nonsense,' he said. 'How could it do so? There's no hole big enough. I told Adder that, but you know Adder.'

Mossy did not. He had never associated with the snake in a personal way, nor did he want to. He did not like snakes at all and could not understand how Badger had made a friend of one. However, he was about to make a remark on the existence of a very large hole he had heard about, when there was a deafening roar. Both Mossy and Badger froze. Mossy's blood nearly curdled in his veins as the scream rent the outside air. The vibrations of the terrible sound seemed to echo through the maze of passages surrounding them. They turned to each other.

'The Beast!' they whispered together.

'That must be its h-hunting c-call,' Mossy stammered.

'I hope all our friends are safely at home,' said Badger. 'What a horrible cry.'

When Mossy had recovered himself he remembered what he had been going to say. 'The hole,' he said, and then had to stop again. He was still quivering.

'The hole?'

'Yes. My mother – ' Poor Mossy broke off again. He had started to explain that his mother Mirthful had told him of a great hole. Then he recalled that Mirthful could not be his mother, as far as Badger was concerned. Mirthful had been his father's mate. He hesitated. Now what could he say? It was *so* awkward.

'Your mother,' Badger prompted him. 'I've never known you to mention your mother before, Mole.'

'Er – no. What I mean is, the – er – female you called Mirthful – she – er – she told me that there *is* a great chamber underground in the Reserve. She came across it by accident once. She thought it was something the humans must have made.'

Badger drew his breath in sharply. 'Is this true?' he almost snapped at Mossy. All other considerations were forgotten now.

'Yes, quite true. I assure you, Badger.'

'Where? Where is this chamber?'

'I don't know. I've never been there. But – but – it can't be far from here. My – er – that is, Mirthful – she lived around here before she – er – mated.'

'Then we must find it,' said Badger. 'And when we've found it . . . ' he stopped and pondered, then he finished lamely, 'we'll know if the Cat uses it.'

'Oh dear. What if the Cat is there when we find it?' Mossy asked tremulously.

'We only have to *see* it,' Badger growled. 'I'll do the seeing. You only have to find the chamber.'

'But – but – '

'No "buts", Mole. This is our very last chance. You're the greatest tunneller of us all. If anybody can find it, you can. Then you can come back to me, tell me where it's situated and I'll go overland. I'll go by day. The Cat will be asleep perhaps. I make a noise' – Badger was enacting the scene in his mind – 'it wakes up. It sees me. I see the Cat. I tell it so – and the threat is removed. The Cat leaves White Deer Park.' He looked at Mossy triumphantly.

'You make it sound very simple,' said the little animal. 'Are you sure there's no more of a risk than that?'

'Only to me,' said Badger, 'and what does that matter? My days are numbered.'

'Oh, Badger,' Mossy pleaded, 'don't start on that again.'

'Very well. I'll say no more,' he answered. 'But I'm relying on you. You're the one now that the whole population of the Reserve depends on, whether they realize it or not.'

Mossy gulped. He did not know if he was equal to such a tremendous responsibility. 'I – I'll do my best,' he said, not very happily. 'I can't do more than that.'

'Of course you can't,' Badger assured him. 'But I know what "best" means for the most efficient of all tunnel travellers. Off with you now. There's no time to lose.'

Mossy scurried away. How was he to begin this impossible task?

He headed first of all for his own comfortable nest where, he was pretty sure, he had left some immobilized worms uneaten. He was glad to find that indeed this was the case. Whilst he was chewing on these, he tried very hard to think of all that Mirthful had told him about the great chamber. The network of underground passages used by his parents was all around him. Many of them he still used himself. In addition to these were some others that his mother had used before she had become mate to his father. Somewhere the two systems connected, because it had been at that point where his parents had first encountered each other. Mossy knew roughly in what direction this place would be, and so that must be the first stage of his exploration. Afterwards he would have to reconnoitre the old tunnels used by Mirthful, in the hope that one of them would bring him to the chamber he sought. He ate a last worm in a pensive sort of way and set off.

He found the connecting point without trouble and ran along the first passage. This led into another and that one into a further passage and it was remarkable, he thought, how free of debris they had remained in all this time. One passage came to a dead end and there, at the end of it, was the remains of an old nest. The materials – dry grass and leaves – had not yet disintegrated entirely. Mossy paused. A feeling of sweet but distant sadness stole over him. He had stumbled across one of his mother's old resting-places.

But there was no time for sentimentality. Underneath the nest was a bolt-hole. Mossy pulled himself into it and simply followed his nose. And it was his nose that was starting to cause problems. Along the passages the scent of earthworms pervaded the damp, close air. Their little burrows were everywhere and often they dropped unsuspectingly into a mole's tunnel. Mossy was having the utmost difficulty in ignoring the sensations picked up by his nose. Although he had eaten recently, he already felt hungry again. He tried to remember the importance of his mission, but the worms intruded more and more into his awareness and, eventually he was unable to resist any longer. He snapped at one and ate it hurriedly. Then he moved on, collecting one here, one there, and stopping each time to devour it. Without realizing it, his journey of exploration had become a worm hunt. He was so intent on satisfying his voracious appetite that he lost all idea of time, where he was going, and what he was meant to be doing. In the midst of grabbing a particularly plump worm from the earth walls, he suddenly seemed to lose his footing. The loose soil gave way beneath him and he found himself plunging down as if into a void. Then there was a bump as he landed abruptly at the bottom.

Luckily he had fallen on to more earth and he was more shaken by the surprise than the severity of the fall. Mossy pulled himself together. A dim light enabled him to see a little. He soon noticed a patch of daylight, like a round piece of whiteness against the mass of black. He knew it was from there that the feeble light filtered through, and he guessed it was a large entrance hole. Then, with a start, he realized where he was. He was in a sort of cavern. Out there, beyond the patch of daylight, lay the Park. Mossy had found the great chamber!

Now he was very frightened. The passage he had fallen from was high up the cavern wall and there was no way by which he could climb back up to it. The only way out was through the main entrance hole. But how could he get to it and out of it safely when the Cat might arrive at any moment? Then his heart turned over. The Cat might even now be inside the cavern, only a few steps away. He did not know – yet. Mossy held himself very still. His heart hammered wildly at the thought. He tried to test the dank air for animal scents, wrinkling his snout all around. There *was* a smell – a warm, sharp sort of smell, which was almost certainly given off by the animal's body. Mossy began to tremble uncontrollably. He could scarcely prevent his teeth from chattering with fright. How he wished someone else were there – Badger preferably – to suggest what he should do. Then he recalled that *he* had to report to Badger. He had to get out into the Park – somehow – so that he could describe the location of the chamber.

Mossy tried to calm himself. Even if an animal *was* present somewhere near him in that cavern, it might be something smaller and less ferocious than the Cat. So he argued to himself. But it was no use. He *knew*, without actually seeing it, that it was the Cat. Now he had two options. One was to try and creep to the exit without being noticed. He did not know if he had the courage to do that. The other was to wait, still and noiseless, until darkness fell again, and hope that the Beast would itself leave on a hunting trip. What an ordeal that would be. It was a good thing he had eaten well. But supposing he waited – how many more lives, perhaps of those whom he knew, would be lost if the Cat rampaged around again? If he could get out now he could prevent this happening.

There was no sound. Was the Cat sleeping or wakeful? At any rate, his – Mossy's – abrupt entry into the chamber did not seem to have been detected. So if his presence was not suspected already, a small animal like himself could have a fair chance of remaining unseen. Keeping close to the side of the chamber, Mossy moved a few centimetres. Then he froze, waiting for a reaction. There was none. He moved a little farther; then farther still in the direction of the disc of daylight. Oh, it seemed so far away. This cavern was really enormous.

Mossy reached a point along the wall where he got, as it were, behind the shaft of faint light that shone into the murky interior. Now he could see part of the chamber quite well where the light fell. And there he saw four huge tawny legs, belonging to a body the rest of which remained in shadow. It was obvious, from the position of the legs, that the body was lying on its side. Evidently the Cat slept. Mossy was encouraged. But he could not resist pausing to peer for a long time, through his weak eyes, at the impressive sight. He compared the huge paws with his own diminutive ones and this set him scuttling on his way again. The exit was closer now and the daylight seemed to be dimming. He could see foliage beyond – thick encompassing foliage that hid the entrance to the chamber from those abroad in the Park. Mossy moved on, nearer and nearer, still keeping as quiet and slow as he could. When he was about two metres from regaining the Park, he heard a stir behind him. The Cat had woken and was stretching its limbs where it lay. There was a muffled growl and Mossy thought he was discovered. He waited, almost dead with fright. But nothing happened. After a while, he started on again. He was nearly there. A breeze blew from ouside and wafted into the chamber, ruffling the Cat's fur. Some dust must have blown into its nostrils, too. Mossy heard a tremendous sneeze. Then the Cat was up and padding towards him. He tried to hurry but it was no use. The Cat, on its long legs, was there before him.

He was seen. The Cat growled softly. Mossy could think of only one thing to do. 'You're seen!' he cried. 'I see you!'

It might have been that the shrill squeaks of the little mole were more or less inaudible to the Cat, or it might have been that the great beast saw Mossy as a welcome extra morsel after the previous night's bad hunting. Either way it paid no attention to his feeble challenge, except to extend one vast paw to pull him close.

Somehow Mossy managed to circumvent the paw and he scurried out of the chamber and began to dig frantically at the soil outside. He was a lightning fast digger and, with three heaves, his head and front paws and half his body had disappeared to safety. He tore at the earth in fury, pulling his body after him, down, down and down into the familiar territory of darkness that enveloped him like a caress.

The Cat was not to be outdone, however. It saw where the tiny animal had gone and set about digging after him. It ripped up clods of the soft soil, scrabbling with both front paws in an angry fit of exasperaton. Mossy could hear the thunder above him and dug down deeper. But the Cat's paws were gaining.

A witness of the struggle flew desparately to help. The miserable and sleepless Tawny Owl was now brave Mossy's only hope.

Tawny Owl had been perched on a branch, away from his friends, unhappily contemplating the prospect of further deaths in the community. He had tried in vain to doze in the sunlight, although for a time he kept his eyes firmly shut. At last he gave up and when he opened his eyes he saw, at a distance, the Cat emerge from the midst of a thick bush and begin digging determinedly. Owl was too far away to have seen the small body of Mossy but he knew, better than any creature, that it was now time for the Cat to honour its pledge.

He launched himself into the air and flew swiftly to a nearby tree. Then, at the top of his voice, he cried, 'I CAN SEE YOU, CAT!'

The animal stopped its digging momentarily and looked around. When it spied Tawny Owl it snarled angrily. Owl quivered but held on. The respite allowed Mossy to tunnel deeper and get farther away.

Tawny Owl noted the Cat made no move. There was a look of fury on its face at being discovered. Owl said, 'You said I'd never see you again. You were wrong. I think you – er – must yield now.'

'YIELD?' the Cat roared terrifyingly. 'To an owl?'

'You gave your word,' Tawny Owl whispered, barely

able to speak. He guessed the pledge was worthless and that now there was no hope for any of them.

The Cat roared again, making the ground vibrate with the din. Badger had heard the first roar and had run to his set entrance in alarm. He had regretted sending the tiny mole on such a dangerous exploration and now he looked around for him in desperation. When the second roar rang out he could stand still no longer. He started to run towards the sound.

By the time he could see the Cat, the animal was digging again and Badger surmised immediately what it was digging for.

'Oh Mole,' he cried to himself in anguish and he increased his pace. Now he noticed Tawny Owl. 'Owl, Owl,' he called breathlessly. 'Do something!'

'It's no use,' the bird wailed. 'We're helpless. The Beast has broken its promise.'

Badger lumbered up, panting but filled with resolution.

'Leave that worthless morsel,' he gasped, putting himself in front of the Cat. 'What good is that mouthful to you? *I'm* more fitted to your appetite. Let me take his place.'

The Cat paused. It turned round and, with a malicious glare, stared at Badger in the fading daylight with undisguised contempt.

'Feeble, powerless weaklings,' it spat at him. 'I could slay *all* of you!'

Badger quailed, despite his determination. Tawny Owl watched in agony on his branch. What *could* he do?

The Cat's eyes blazed with the intensity of living fire. Suddenly a roar, like a distant echo of the Cat's, could be heard far away. The Beast's majestic head snapped round, its ears pricking up erect as sentinels. The sound was repeated on a higher note. In an instant the Cat forgot about Badger, Tawny Owl and the hidden Mossy and, in the failing light, lifted up its head and roared deafeningly. The call was answered, now not so distant. The Cat leapt up gracefully, clearing all the surrounding obstacles with ease, and bounded away through the trees.

Badger and Tawny Owl, the two old friends, looked at each other hesitantly. Was there *another* of the Beasts? As they held their silence, more roars could be heard, the one answering the other. Now more Park animals began to make themselves seen, asking each other what these awful sounds portended.

Badger said quietly to Tawny Owl, 'Let's go back and mix with the others. Mole will make his own way home.'

Now Tawny Owl understood about the digging. He made no comment on Badger's use of the name 'Mole'.

They found Fox and Vixen and Weasel in a cheerful mood that contrasted strangely with their own.

'Why such long faces?' Weasel chided them. 'This is cause for celebration.'

'Celebration?' Badger muttered. 'How can you – ' He broke off. A light seemed to penetrate his thoughts. 'Can it be?' he asked himself. And then he heard it. The cries of hundreds of birds, chirping and singing joyfully.

'Oh tell me, Weasel – Fox – someone – tell me what you think,' begged Badger.

'Those roars can mean only one thing,' said Weasel. 'The Cat has been called away. It's still spring. That could only be the call of a female crying for a mate!'

The roars were becoming fainter and, as they listened, dusk began to descend.

'Yes,' said Fox. 'It seems that what we've striven for so

hopelessly all along, has now been achieved by an outside influence.'

The birds were still singing. The animals thrilled at the sound. They were crying, 'It's left the Park! It's left the Park!'

Epilogue

During the last few days of spring the animals could not quite believe their Park had been returned to them. The Farthing Wood community had listened to Mossy's description of the cavern, and they had gone to the spot to look at the entrance behind the thick bushes that concealed it. Fox and Vixen had even scrambled inside to look. But the grisly remains of the Beast's last meals had soon prompted their return to fresher air. They told none of the others what they had seen.

Some of the birds who had so gladly broadcast the Cat's departure had not been satisfied with that alone. They had flown into open country to follow the route it took. They saw the other Cat that had called it away – a slightly smaller beast, but equally powerful in their eyes. And this one's power did not extend merely to strength. With some surprise, the birds watched the excited meeting of the two Cats. For the smaller animal appeared to dominate the great creature that had terrorized the Park. Wherever she led, the male followed. She called to him frequently as they went and, almost with a sort of meekness, he was content to do her bidding. He ambled in her wake quite happily, and such was their stride that they were soon a long way from the Reserve. It was apparent that the female's territory was in quite another area. Eventually the birds returned home with the news.

One of them remarked that 'it was as if the Beast had been tamed'.

So the roars and screams of the great Cat were heard no more in White Deer Park. The animals' lives resumed an ordinariness that at times seemed almost dull by its comparison with the frights and fears they had endured for so long.

'It almost seems now,' Friendly remarked to his father, 'that the danger we faced day after day added a sort of zest to our existence.'

Fox disagreed. 'When you reach my time of life,' he replied, 'what you call "zest" is something you only want to recall in your memories. And Vixen and I have plenty of those.'

Soon Squirrel came back to the fold and the group of old friends was more or less complete again.

The opinions of the older creatures – Badger, Tawny Owl, Weasel, Toad and Whistler – tallied with those of Fox. They looked forward to nothing more than a period of peace to enjoy for as long as they were able to gather together. But the opinion of one old friend was not known, and that was Adder's. He had not put in an appearance since the siege of the Nature Reserve had been lifted. Only Leveret had seen him since that time, and the snake's excuse had been, as usual, a cryptic one. His remark had puzzled Leveret who had passed it on to the others, hoping for some enlightenment. There was none offered. They were as mystified as he. For Adder had merely referred to the fact that he had recently become interested 'in a new association'.

The summer waxed and waned and the chill of autumn crackled with the clash of antlers of the stags in the white deer herd. The Great Stag had many rivals now and had more difficulty than ever before in holding his place. The fawns who had survived the ravages of the stranger's raids had grown too, and eventually the leadership would be passed on, perhaps many seasons hence, to one of these. Whatever happened, the herd that had given the Park its name would still be there, stepping gracefully through the woods and grassland of the Nature Reserve.

Another winter beckoned. Deep in his set, with a thick pile of bedding around him, Badger wondered if it would be his last. His old bones were beginning to ache with age and the cold, and he found himself thinking again about his ancient system of tunnels in Farthing Wood. In a soft, rather feeble but warm voice he said to Mossy, who was visiting, 'It was a wonderful set, Mole. Do you remember the Assembly, when the whole Wood gathered in my home to talk?'

'Oh yes,' said Mossy. 'I remember. I wonder what Farthing Wood is like now?'

Other great reads **from Red Fox**

Further Red Fox titles that you might enjoy reading are listed on the following pages. They are available in bookshops or they can be ordered directly from us.

If you would like to order books, please send this form and the money due to:

ARROW BOOKS, BOOKSERVICE BY POST, PO BOX 29, DOUGLAS, ISLE OF MAN, BRITISH ISLES. Please enclose a cheque or postal order made out to Arrow Books Ltd for the amount due, plus 75p per book for postage and packing to a maximum of £7.50, both for orders within the UK. For customers outside the UK, please allow £1.00 per book.

NAME_____

ADDRESS_____

_____

Please print clearly.

Whilst every effort is made to keep prices low, it is sometimes necessary to increase cover prices at short notice. If you are ordering books by post, to save delay it is advisable to phone to confirm the correct price. The number to ring is THE SALES DEPARTMENT 071 (if outside London) 973 9700.

Other great reads from **Red Fox**

Discover the great animal stories of Colin Dann

JUST NUFFIN

The Summer holidays loomed ahead with nothing to look forward to except one dreary week in a caravan with only Mum and Dad for company. Roger was sure he'd be bored.

But then Dad finds Nuffin: an abandoned puppy who's more a bundle of skin and bones than a dog. Roger's holiday is transformed and he and Nuffin are inseparable. But Dad is adamant that Nuffin must find a new home. Is there *any* way Roger can persuade him to change his mind?

ISBN 0 09 966900 5   £2.99

KING OF THE VAGABONDS

'You're very young,' Sammy's mother said, 'so heed my advice. Don't go into Quartermile Field.'

His mother and sister are happily domesticated but Sammy, the tabby cat, feels different. They are content with their lot, never wondering what lies beyond their immediate surroundings. But Sammy is burningly curious and his life seems full of mysteries. Who is his father? Where has he gone? And what is the mystery of Quartermile Field?

ISBN 0 09 957190 0   £2.99

Other great reads from **Red Fox**

Enter the gripping world of the REDWALL saga

REDWALL   Brian Jacques

It is the start of the summer of the Late Rose. Redwall Abbey, the peaceful home of a community of mice, slumbers in the warmth of a summer afternoon.

But not for long. Cluny is coming! The evil one-eyed rat warlord is advancing with his battle-scarred mob. And Cluny wants Redwall . . .

ISBN 0 09 951200 9   £3.99

MOSSFLOWER   Brian Jacques

One late autumn evening, Bella of Brockhall snuggled deep in her armchair and told a story . . .

This is the dramatic tale behind the bestselling *Redwall*. It is the gripping account of how Redwall Abbey was founded through the bravery of the legendary mouse Martin and his epic quest for Salmandastron.

ISBN 0 09 955400 3   £3.99

MATTIMEO   Brian Jacques

Slagar the fox is intent on revenge . . .

On bringing death and destruction to the inhabitants of Redwall Abbey, in particular to the fearless warrior mouse Matthias. His cunning and cowardly plan is to steal the Redwall children—and Mattimeo, Matthias' son, is to be the biggest prize of all.

ISBN 0 09 967540 4   £3.99

MARIEL OF REDWALL   Brian Jacques

Brian Jacques starts his second trilogy about Redwall Abbey with the adventures of the mousemaid Mariel, lost and betrayed by Slagar the Fox, but fighting back with all her spirit.

ISBN 0 09 992960 0   £4.50

Other great reads *from* **Red Fox**

Discover the wacky world of Spacedog and Roy by Natalie Standiford

Spacedog isn't really a dog at all – he's an alien lifeform from the planet Queekrg, who just happens to *look* like a dog. It's a handy form of disguise – but he's not sure he'll *ever* get used to the food!

SPACEDOG AND ROY

Roy is quite surprised to find an alien spacecraft in his garden – but that's nothing to the surprise he gets when Spacedog climbs out.

ISBN 0 09 983650 5   £2.99

SPACEDOG AND THE PET SHOW

Life becomes unbearable for Spacedog when he's entered for the local pet show and a French poodle falls in love with him.

ISBN 0 09 983660 2   £2.99

SPACEDOG IN TROUBLE

When Spacedog is mistaken for a stray and locked up in the animal santuary, he knows he's in big trouble.

ISBN 0 09 983670 X   £2.99

SPACEDOG THE HERO

When Roy's father goes away he makes Spacedog the family watchdog – but Spacedog is scared of the dark. What can he do?

ISBN 0 09 983680 7   £2.99

Join the RED FOX Reader's Club

The Red Fox Reader's Club is for readers of all ages. All you have to do is ask your local bookseller or librarian for a Red Fox Reader's Club card. As an official Red Fox Reader you only have to borrow or buy eight Red Fox books in order to qualify for your own Red Fox Reader's Clubpack – full of exciting surprises! If you have any difficulty obtaining a Red Fox Reader's Club card please write to: Random House Children's Books Marketing Department, 20 Vauxhall Bridge Road, London SW1V 2SA.